CHARMED PLACES

Hudson River Artists and Their Houses, Studios, and Vistas

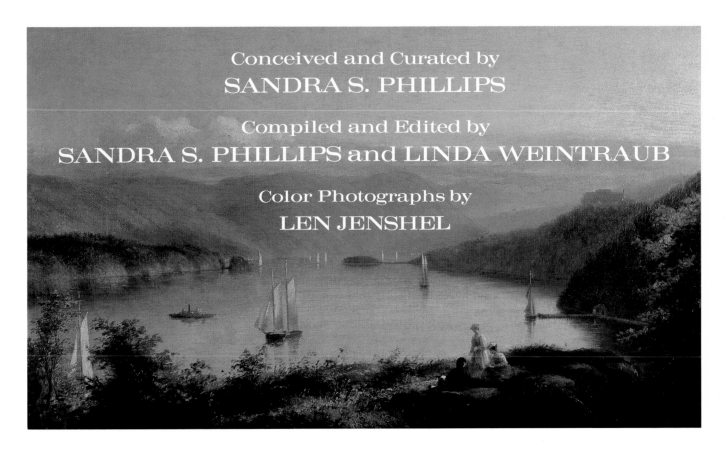

Conceived and Curated by
SANDRA S. PHILLIPS

Compiled and Edited by
SANDRA S. PHILLIPS and **LINDA WEINTRAUB**

Color Photographs by
LEN JENSHEL

WITH ESSAYS BY

□ JAMES MARSTON FITCH □ ALBERT FEIN □ DONELSON HOOPES □

SANDRA S. PHILLIPS □ WILLIAM RHOADS

THE EDITH C. BLUM INSTITUTE, BARD COLLEGE AND
THE VASSAR COLLEGE ART GALLERY

IN ASSOCIATION WITH

HARRY N. ABRAMS, INC., PUBLISHERS, NEW YORK

PROJECT MANAGER: BEVERLY FAZIO
COPY EDITOR: JANET WILSON
DESIGNER: CAROL ROBSON

EXHIBITION ITINERARY

Edith C. Blum Art Institute, Bard College, Anandale-on-Hudson, N.Y., April 17–August 17, 1988
Vassar College Art Gallery, Poughkeepsie, N.Y., April 17–August 28, 1988
Albany Institute of History and Art, September 28–November 6, 1988
The Queens Museum, Flushing, N.Y., January 22–March 5, 1989
The Hudson River Museum, Yonkers, N.Y., March 19–June 11, 1989

Front cover: Len Jenshel.
View Toward Hudson River from the Porch at Olana,
House of Frederic E. Church, Hudson, N.Y. (cat. no. 41)

Back cover: Robert Havell, Jr.
View of the Hudson River from near Sing Sing (cat. no. 22)

Page 3: Robert W. Weir.
View of the Hudson River from West Point (cat. no. 4)

Library of Congress Cataloging-in-Publication Data
Charmed places.
Bibliography: p. 156
Includes index.
1. Hudson River school of landscape painting.
2. Landscape painters—Homes and haunts—Hudson River
Valley (N.Y. and N.J.)   3. Hudson River Valley
(N.Y. and N.J.) in art.   4. Landscape painting—19th
century—Hudson River Valley (N.Y. and N.J.)
I. Phillips, Sandra S., 1945–   .   II. Weintraub,
Linda.   III. Title.
ND1351.5.C47   1988   758'.1'097473   87–72079
ISBN 0–8109–1041–1

CONTENTS

Albert Bierstadt
VIEW ON THE HUDSON LOOKING ACROSS THE TAPPAN ZEE TOWARDS HOOK MOUNTAIN
1866. Oil on canvas, 36¼ x 72¼"
Courtesy 1987 Sotheby's, Inc., New York

LENDERS TO THE EXHIBITION

Albany Institute of History and Art

Allen Memorial Art Museum, Oberlin College, Ohio

Archives of American Art, Smithsonian Institution, Washington, D.C.

Berkshire Museum, Pittsfield, Mass.

Mr. and Mrs. Herbert Baer Brill

Julia L. Butterfield Memorial Library, Cold Spring, N.Y.

Cleveland Museum of Art

Columbia County Historical Society, Kinderhook, N.Y.

Cooper-Hewitt Museum, Smithsonian Institution, New York

Detroit Institute of Art

Joyce Randall Edwards, Dobbs Ferry, N.Y.

Hastings Historical Society, N.Y.

Nelson-Atkins Museum of Art, Kansas City, Mo.

Newington-Cropsey Foundation, Hastings-on-Hudson, N.Y.

New-York Historical Society, New York

New York Public Library, New York

New York State Library, Albany

New York State Museum, Albany

New York State Office of Parks, Recreation and Historic Preservation,
Olana State Historic Site, Hudson, N.Y.

Onteora Club, N.Y.

Ossining Historical Society, N.Y.

Kaycee Benton Parra

The Rev. and Mrs. DeWolf Perry

Preservation Society of Newport County, Newport, R.I.

Putnam County Historical Society, Cold Spring, N.Y.

Fred Radl, New Paltz, N.Y.

Anne Armstrong Rice

Professor and Mrs. William B. Rhoads

Theodore Kensett Rossiter

Mr. and Mrs. Herbert L. Shultz

Edith Cole Silberstein

United States Military Academy Library, West Point, N.Y.

West Point Museum Collections, United States Military Academy

Vassar College Art Gallery, Poughkeepsie, N.Y.

Vassar College Library

Mr. and Mrs. Verne Vance

The Wadsworth Atheneum, Hartford, Conn.

Yale University Art Gallery, New Haven, Conn.

Young-Morse Historic Site, Poughkeepsie, N.Y.

Private Collection

FOREWORD AND ACKNOWLEDGMENTS

In 1982 I received a telephone call from Eric Egas and Kay Stamer, former executive director of the Greene County Council on the Arts and his successor. They wanted me to advise them on a project they called "Lives and Studios," consisting of documentary material about artists—from Thomas Cole to modern painters—who lived in Greene County and nearby areas. From the wide variety of photographs, letters, and other items they had collected, it was evident even then that the nineteenth-century painters of this general area showed a marked interest in their houses and studios, and that some of their aesthetic concerns were reflected in the sites they chose or in the style of their buildings. In other words, these artists had used their environment as part of their artistic expression. I proposed a project to study this phenomenon, and we received a planning grant from the New York State Council on the Arts to start research on what we called "Artists and Their Environments" and later, more appropriately, "Charmed Places."

What we discovered was the correspondence between the end of the Classical Revival in architectural history and the beginning of the alternative picturesque styles, which these artists both reflected and in a sense participated in. In the earlier period, buildings were white, geometric, and ordered; nature was seen as chaos needing to be disciplined—much as the gardens at Versailles were plotted in clear, intellectual, and regular patterns, in great contrast to the irregularity of the natural growth of plants. By the time Cole moved to Catskill, however, a change had occurred. A resident of Newburgh, Andrew Jackson Downing, was Cole's contemporary, and his bracketed cottages, painted in colors harmonious with nature, were irregular, picturesque, and sought harmony with, not distance from, the surrounding environment. Landscapes were "natural"—more in keeping with the so-called English style of landscaping of Capability Brown and others like him. Nature and man complemented and reflected each other. The sensitivity of these artists to landscape and architecture arose from this changed sensibility. Although the Hudson River School artists had been studied, and also Neo-Gothic developments in architecture and landscape design, the similarity of the artists' ideas and expression to those of the architects and landscape architects would become clear from directly experiencing the houses, studios, gardens, and vistas of these nineteenth-century artists—a "natural" pursuit for an art historian living in the area.

Thanks are due first to the Greene County Council on the Arts, through which this project received its initial support, with both grant sponsorship and enthusiastic moral support. I would also like to thank those scholars who took an early interest in this project and advised me: Milton W. Brown, Alf Evers, Linda S. Ferber, and William H. Gerdts, Jr. James Marston Fitch has been so supportive that he wished to be a participant. Linda Weintraub, director of the Edith C. Blum Art Institute at Bard College, was supportive of this project at a crucial stage and assisted me greatly in its realization as an exhibition—first at Bard and then jointly with Vassar; Jan E. Adlmann, director of the Vassar College Art Gallery, graciously allowed me to work on this exhibition as part of my duties at Vassar.

Many thanks go to those who have helped us in funding the project: Andrea Miron and Mary Schlosser, chair and former chair of the Friends of the Vassar College Art Gallery; Dr. Frances D. Fergusson, president of Vassar College (herself an architectural historian); Joan Davidson of the Kaplan Fund and Barnabas McHenry, formerly of the Lila Acheson Wallace Funds, have been most kind, as have George Lamb of the Jackson Hole

Preserve, the New York State Council on the Arts, the O'Connor Fund, Scenic Hudson, the Newington-Cropsey Foundation, Hudson River Heritage, Howard and Dorothy Pack, Henry Meagher, Ann Morse, the Poughkeepsie Savings Bank, and an anonymous donor.

Others who have contributed information, time, and assistance are: Rebecca Arvidson, my student research intern at Vassar; Tammis Groft and Thomas Nelson of the Albany Institute for History and Art; Lynn S. Beman; Barbara Biszek; Mr. and Mrs. Bertram Blumberg; John Carmichael; Nicolai Cikovsky, Jr.; Sally Bottiggi and Ruth Piwonka of the Columbia County Historical Society; Dorothy Oakes and Ella Stedner, Cragsmoor Free Library; Wendy Curtis; Tema Harnik, Dobbs Ferry Historical Society; Stephen Ediden; Whitty Sanford, Erpf Catskill Cultural Center; Mrs. Orville de Forest Edwards; Dr. Betsy Fahlman; Margot Hirsch Feely; Pamela Read, The Alice and Hamilton Fish Library; Ilene Susan Fort; E. Davis Gaillard; Barbara Dyer Gallatti; Helen Ver Nooy Gearn; the staff at the Greene County Council on the Arts, which received the NYSCA Planning Grant and the O'Connor Foundation; Raymond Beecher, Shelby Kriele, and Mabel Parker Smith, Greene County Historical Society; Mary L. Allison, Hastings Historical Society; Justine Hommel, Haines Falls Free Library; Nat Hendricks; Eric and Peggy Lasry; David Leveson; Karen Lucic; Brian Lukacher; Kenneth W. Maddox; Bannon McHenry; Suzanne Boorsch, Maria Morris Hambourg, and David Kiehl, The Metropolitan Museum of Art; Craig Mowhirt, Francis Murphy; Florence Levins of the Newington-Cropsey Foundation; Lawrence and Donna Newton; Kaycee Benton Parra; James Ryan, Olana State Historic Site; Mary Tynes of the Onteora Park Library; Roberta Y. Arminio, Ossining Historical Society; Howard and Dorothy Pack; Elwood C. Parry III; Mrs. Robert P. Patterson; the Rev. DeWolf Perry; Irma W. Franklin and Jean B. Rosenwald, Putnam County Historical Society; Maureen Radl; John Reboul; Nancy Rice; Theodore K. Rossiter; Martica Sawin; John Scott; Leigh Jones, Senate House Historic Site; Mrs. John Seredensky; Mr. and Mrs. Herbert Schultz; Edith Cole Silberstein; Hollee Haswell, Sleepy Hollow Restorations; Ruth Nenendorffer and Adelaide Smith of the Historical Society of the Tarrytowns; Marie Capps and Michael Moss, United States Military Academy at West Point; Mr. and Mrs. Verne Vance; Robert C. Vose, Jr.; Mr. and Mrs. Alan T. Wenzell; Ila Weiss; Timothy Countryman, Young-Morse Historic Site; Mr. and Mrs. Arnold Zellner; and Alice Zigelis.

Finally I would like to thank my friends and family, who have patiently endured years of this project, and without whom it would never have become a reality.

Sandra S. Phillips

Thomas Cole
MOUNT MERINO, NEAR HUDSON
c. 1835. Oil on canvas, 33 x 45″
Courtesy of Berry-Hill Galleries, New York

It is a privilege to celebrate a national art tradition that originated in one's own neighborhood. It is a special privilege to have an opportunity to generate new information related to this tradition. "Charmed Places" combines both; it focuses attention, for the first time, on the home and studio environments of the long-admired members of the Hudson River School. These architectural treasures have never before been the subject of study. As a result, the importance of this project extends far beyond the usual parameters of even the most successful exhibitions. In addition to providing the first opportunity to study the works of art and archival material documenting the sites in which these famed nineteenth-century artists lived, the exhibition will, it is hoped, alert the owners of these properties to the fact that their homes have historic importance and therefore demand special respect.

The Hudson River Valley was the first great center of American picturesque architecture and landscape gardening. The Hudson River painters participated in this movement. They took an active interest in designing their rural houses and studios. The records that survive, as well as the sites themselves, enhance our understanding of each artist's aesthetic concerns and philosophies. They demonstrate that sensitivity to the environment is not only a contemporary concern. The regional artists of the nineteenth century established a true and noble ancestry for the artistic and conservation ideals that prevail today. The eloquent beauty and variety of Hudson River Valley scenery continues to inspire artists and residents today, just as it did in the preceding century. Perhaps we should acknowledge the contribution made by these artists in first recognizing that this region is very special and worthy of our attention.

The project has absorbed the talents and energies of innumerable participants. I would like to thank Kay Stamer of the Greene County Council on the Arts for inviting Bard College to participate in this exciting undertaking. Sandra S. Phillips has conducted the curatorial efforts with extraordinary skill and perseverance. Richard Wiles, James Marston Fitch, Donelson Hoopes, William Rhoads, and Albert Fein each contributed vital new scholarship to the literature on nineteenth-century architecture and art. Joann Potter, Elaine Ring, Judy Samoff, Ann Gabler, Catherine Egenberger, Jonathan Feldschuk, Jamie Monagan all contributed their special talents to fulfilling the potential of this project. And, of course, special gratitude is extended to each of the lenders and donors who not only shared our conviction that this was a very worthwhile project but who chose to help make it a reality.

Linda Weintraub
Director,
Edith C. Blum Art Institute,
Bard College

Jasper F. Cropsey
VIEW OF THE HUDSON FROM THE ARTIST'S HOME. 1887
Oil on canvas, 7 x 10″
Newington-Cropsey Foundation, Hastings-on-Hudson, N.Y.

1. Asher B. Durand. KINDRED SPIRITS. 1849

Oil on canvas, 46 x 36″

Astor, Lenox, and Tilden Foundations, New York Public Library

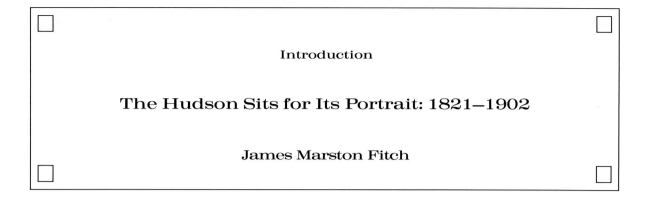

Introduction

The Hudson Sits for Its Portrait: 1821–1902

James Marston Fitch

The Hudson is one of several great American rivers, like the Ashley at Charleston or the Mississippi at New Orleans, that developed a great metropolis where it flowed into the sea. The Hudson shared many of the characteristics of these other riverine systems. Each drained a vast hinterland, first of primeval forests, then of farms and small-scale mills and mines, and finally, toward the end of the nineteenth century, of farms, towns, and industry. But each evolved a distinctive society along its banks, partly as a result of variations in climate and topography, partly as a result of the vast difference between two social systems, one slave-powered and one free.

One of the consequences of this difference is that the Hudson produced a great school of painters, while the southern streams produced none at all. One might almost say that the lower reaches of these rivers were too stupefyingly monotonous for the artist to *see*, much less to isolate and organize their landscape features into painterly compositions. On the other hand, the sheer topography of the Hudson—flanked by terraces backed up with mountains and dramatically intersected by palisades and escarpments—fell naturally into an endless series of picturesque compositions. But onto this natural landscape, by the time the painters began to arrive in the 1820s, there had already been superimposed a two-hundred-year accumulation of farms, orchards, villages, and manorial estates. It was this dazzling juxtaposition of God-made and man-made that perfectly met the Victorian requirement for a mix of the sublime and the beautiful, the wild and the tamed.

The discovery of the beauties of the natural American landscape by American artists and tourists came at just about the time when a safe and relaxed contemplation of the wilderness became possible: that is to say, at the beginning of the nineteenth century. Before that time, the forest primeval had been too close and omnipresent, too fraught with real and imagined terrors, too difficult to travel to or dangerous to pass through, to encourage poetry or painting in the plein air. Audubon could not sketch the avian beauties of Trans Appalachia nor James Fenimore Cooper celebrate the noble savage until Daniel Boone had laid the basis for "taming" both.

With the invention of the steam engine, the pioneers were speedily followed into the wilderness by the river steamboat and the railroad. Fulton's first steamboat took twenty-eight hours and forty-five minutes on its run from New York City to Albany in 1811; by 1836 this was down to nine hours and ten minutes; there were night boats to Albany and daytime locals with many stops up and down the river. Fares ranged from twenty cents to Yonkers to $1.50 to Albany. The first railroad up the Valley was completed to Albany in 1845. Thus it was easy enough for the painters, most of whom were New York–based, to reach any point in the Valley. Of course the initial impulse for such transportation systems was commercial, not touristic: to move cattle, grain, timber, and the like down to Manhattan and the sea, and to move finished goods up from the coastal cities, the East Coast, and Europe. In this respect, development along the Hudson would have differed little from that along other American rivers, but the sheer scenographic splendors of the Valley gave rise to a parallel phenomenon: the rise of modern tourism, of people who traveled on the same boats and trains only "to see the sights."

This riverine landscape, which was the focus of both painterly and touristic attention, extended without interruption from Manhattan to Albany and beyond. It was dominated, both culturally and visually, by the estates of the gentry. Chronologically these extended from the estates of the earliest Dutch patroons—Phillipses at Tarrytown, Van Cortlandts at Croton, Van Rensselaers at Albany—through the huge Livingston clan

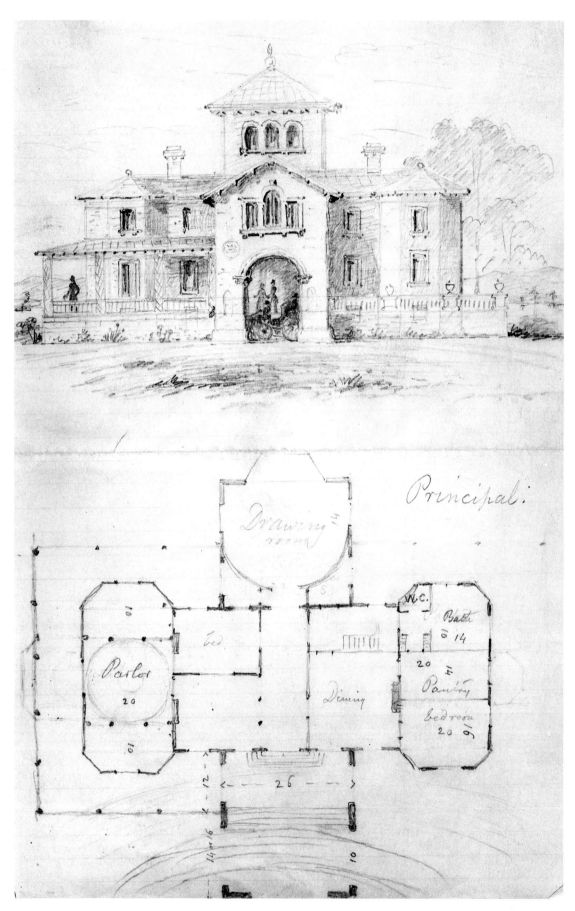

2. Samuel F. B. Morse. LOCUST GROVE, FRONTAL VIEW. c. 1849
Pencil on paper, 8 x 12½″
Young-Morse Historic Site, N.Y.

with their great classic mansions Montgomery Place, Edgewater, and Clermont, down to the great houses being built by post–Civil War commuters like Jay Gould at Tarrytown and William Vanderbilt at Hyde Park. Although these estates did not literally encompass all the land of the Valley, they dominated its physical development and provided its "tone." Topographically their manicured grounds and the surrounding orchards and farmlands offered the contrast with natural features of mountains and palisades so essential to landscape painting like that of the Hudson River School.

And culturally this riverine gentry was, if not friendly, then not actively hostile to the painters, though there is little evidence that it bought much of their work. As William Rhoads's essay in this volume indicates, initially the artists seemed to have thought of themselves as summer visitors, maintaining residences, studios, and galleries in New York City. Gradually they acquired the residences that are the subject of this exhibition. Many of them were modest, at least to begin with—ad hoc affairs, though three of the most pretentious of the Hudson River villas were built by the most pretentious of the painters themselves—Samuel F. B. Morse's Locust Grove (1847), Albert Bierstadt's Malkasten at Tarrytown (1866), and Frederic Church's Olana (begun 1870). These buildings are the subject of this exhibition.

Painting is, after all, a quintessentially urbane activity. Few artists, anxious though they might have been to confront the forest primeval, would have been willing to do so without the domestic comforts of hot meals, clean sheets, and tub baths. They found such amenities all up and down the Valley: at the inns along the river and the post roads, at bed-and-breakfast farmhouses and village boardinghouses, and—after 1828—in such luxurious resort hotels as the Mountain House at Catskill. The great attraction of the Valley, as the scene of a landscapist's activities, was that a hike of only a few miles from their lodgings in the domesticated valley would take them to the "wildest" mountain scenery. Many of the artists found such scenery literally at their front doors. Church would never paint a more majestic sky in the Andes than he did from his own front porch at Olana. And even when, in the latter part of the century, men like him and Bierstadt ventured into the more awesome wildernesses of the Rockies, they did so from the secure and comfortable base of guides and packhorses. The cosmopolitan audiences for whom they painted would have always stood comfortingly behind them.

The authors of the essays in this book—all of them specialists in one or another aspect of Hudson River history—are committed to locating its painters in cultural time and space. From them we learn that the Hudson River School, one of the most powerful regional movements in American art, was overwhelmingly English in its origins. Albert Fein points out in his essay that it was the English who had developed an expertise not only in landscape painting but also in the companion fields of landscape gardening and the literature of landscape theory. And a surprising number of the older men were born and trained in England, according to Sandra Phillips's survey of the artists. Thus the English engraver John Hill was reproducing the landscapes of the English watercolorist William Guy Wall: both had emigrated to the Valley in the 1820s. Robert Havell, the English engraver of Audubon's prints, and another English painter, George Harvey, came to the Valley at about the same time. And Thomas Cole, the so-called founder of the School, was born and trained in England. Professor Rhoads describes the many adaptations of English elements in the artists' houses. These men did much to establish the philosophical and aesthetic armature on which the Hudson River School of painting was to be constructed. Of course the majority of painters would be native-born Americans, and the movement itself became a uniquely American phenomenon.

As a recognizable entity, the School survived until at least 1902, with the establishment of the artists' colony at the old village of Woodstock, outside of the Valley proper. (It could be argued that at Woodstock the movement still lives. But the continuity is more sociological than aesthetic, since the Woodstock painters have long ago been reintegrated into the cosmopolitan mainstream of American art.) The amazing coherence and durability of the idiom itself are in large measure due to the large audience it developed early on. And this audience extended far beyond the conventional gallery and museum system to include the mass reproduction of their works in prints, lithographs, magazines, and books. These created an enormous public appetite not only for the art of the painted river landscapes but for actual touristic experience of the sites themselves.

Although one section of the exhibition consists of an exhilarating collection of painting by the artists of this School, no attempt at a critical evaluation of them is made in this book. Not only have these works been already widely exhibited and written about but they are not directly the subject of this exhibition. Nevertheless, they are important for what they tell us about the mind-set of their makers. Generally the tone is buoyant, sanguine, even when the theme of the individual canvas may be elegiac, even sad. Here nature is seen in all her moods and seasons as being nourishing, supportive, restorative: in the word of that greatest of all Victorian landscapists, Frederick Law Olmsted, *re*-creational.

Architecture does occasionally appear in these canvases but seldom as a central theme—usually as a distant farmhouse here, a riverside village in the middle distance there. This was a truly Claudian use of architecture in the landscape, as ornamental accents like sculpture in the garden. These paintings are suffused with a sense of great things about to happen. A great deal *has* happened in the Valley since the last of these artists painted there, and not all of it has been happy. But the fundamental scenery is too heroic in scale and too durable in structure to have been irremediably damaged by man. And the paintings show the same ineffable permanence. One cannot stand on the northern tip of West Point today and look up the Hudson toward Cold Spring without feeling the same *frisson* of joy and awe which Robert W. Weir must have felt when he painted it in 1854.

3. Thomas Cole. DESIGN FOR A VILLA.
1840—41. Pen, ink, and graphite on paper, 26½ x 19⅜"
The Detroit Institute of Art, Detroit, Mich.
Founders Society Purchase, William H. Murphy Fund
(39.555)

Chapter 1

LANDSCAPE ARCHITECTURE AND THE HUDSON RIVER VALLEY: THE JUNCTURE OF NATURE AND TECHNOLOGY

Albert Fein

Introduction

During the first half of the nineteenth century a widespread commitment to progress through technology paralleled and at times conflicted with a belief in the value of maintaining the environment. Both concepts were basic to the building of the nation and required considerable governmental support. Such involvement, particularly at the state level, was essential for industrial development as well as for obtaining sufficient open space for a rapidly expanding metropolitan society. A young country settling a continent required progressive technology; at the same time, immigrants from many lands, in a nation with neither a long history nor a unifying church, had in nature a common heritage—an ancient past and a manifestation of God and sacred places.[1]

Indeed, in a new democracy that defined itself as different from an older and more aristocratic Europe, the contrasting images of "the machine" and "the garden" were equally important (fig.1). These two characteristics are evident, for example, in the popular appeal of Niagara Falls, an icon of power and beauty. Growing industrialization and commercialization challenged society's capacity to protect a natural heritage identified in rivers, forests, and waterfalls as well as in man-made places such as "rural" cemeteries and public parks.

This dualism was first apparent nationally in the Hudson River Valley. The large-scale application of technology—steam ferry, canal, aqueduct, and railroad (fig.2)—had transformed the Valley, integrating city and countryside into a region stretching from north and west of Albany to New York City. Landscape art was related to this economic, physical, and social development as an extraordinary visual documentation and interpretation of the "nature" of this region—its varied aesthetic qualities—which encompassed the Adirondacks, the Catskills, Niagara Falls, and the White Mountains.[2]

Symbolic of this change was the joining of the two environments inhabited by most of the artists discussed in this exhibition. They had homes in the Valley as well as residences and workplaces in New York City, the nation's major art market. Concerned with the Valley, they were aware that the various places they so lovingly depicted were given regional coherence by a river environment with headwaters in the Adirondacks, flowing to the Atlantic Ocean and terminating as a vital part of New York City's physical fabric. These artists also shared an aesthetic vocabulary including architecture and landscape gardening.[3]

The dominant aesthetic of the period was the picturesque, a generic concept encompassing "the sublime" and "the beautiful," derived from eighteenth-century English theorists and adopted here by the 1830s. In this cultural climate it was logical and still possible for artists such as Thomas Cole (Introduction, fig. 2), Frederic Church (cat. no. 35), and Jasper Cropsey (cat. no. 64) to function as architects of domestic building, especially their own homes. From their careful study of nature, such artists would understandably be familiar with the principles of landscape gardening. It was almost inevitable that efforts would be made to use new techniques to extend the art of designing private gardens into the planning of public landscapes such as "rural" cemeteries and urban parks.

The tension between technology and nature expressed itself in the transition of landscape gardening—one of the major private art forms of the period—into public-oriented landscape architecture. The term "landscape architecture" was not used in this country until 1860, when it was adopted by the codesigners of Central

1. Asher B. Durand. THE FIRST HARVEST IN THE WILDERNESS. 1855
Oil on canvas, 32⅛ x 48¹/₁₆″
The Brooklyn Museum

Park, the nation's first major urban open space, to describe their efforts for the metropolitan region of New York. The designers were the English-born and -educated architect Calvert Vaux (1824–1895) and the American scientific farmer–social reformer Frederick Law Olmsted (1822–1903).[4]

Both men were extending the principles of their mentor, Andrew Jackson Downing (1815–1852), the nation's most popular theorist of architecture and landscape gardening, who urged the development of more public open spaces. The son of working-class parents, Downing was largely self-educated. Gifted, observant, astute, and self-assured, he entered the world of the landed gentry through meeting European aristocrats and through marriage to the granddaughter of John Quincy Adams. The Austrian painter Raphael Hoyle introduced him to the subjects constituting landscape gardening: geology, botany, and aesthetics.[5]

An Anglophile, Downing was committed to the picturesque style of gardening that had evolved in eighteenth-century England, equally evident in urban gardens and rural estates. He was familiar with the writings of John Claudius Loudon, the seminal theorist of landscape gardening, and with the work of the equally renowned English practitioner, Sir Joseph Paxton. As the American correspondent for Loudon's important journal, *Gardeners Magazine,* Downing had expressed his admiration for the Duke of Devonshire's estate, Chatsworth, managed by Paxton, who had contributed noteworthy designs for its architecture, engineering, and landscape. In 1851, in his magazine, *Horticulturist,* Downing presented a favorable account of Paxton's notable design of a public park for the center of England's first planned industrial town, Birkenhead, across the Mersey River from Liverpool. Like Loudon, who promoted parks, and Paxton, who designed them, Downing came to believe that public parks would provide an industrializing and urbanizing democracy with the functional and aesthetic surroundings enjoyed by the landed aristocracy.[6]

Downing considered architecture integral to landscape gardening, an association characteristic of a harmonious society. He believed that a principal challenge to national tranquillity was the mobility of its citizens,

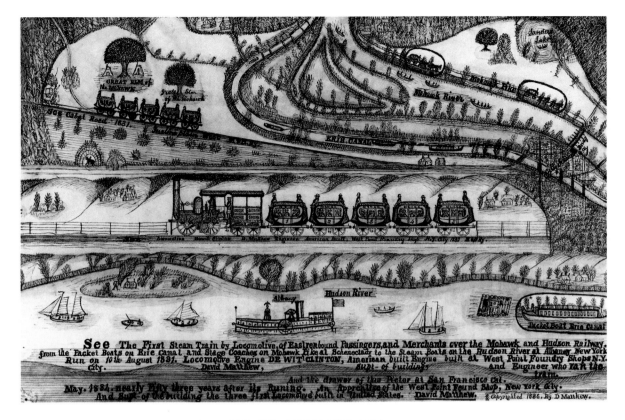

2. David Matthew. THE LOCOMOTIVE "DeWITT CLINTON". 1884
Pen and ink, watercolor on paper, 11 x 17¼"
New-York Historical Society

"the great tendency towards constant change, and the restless spirit of emigration, which form part of our national character; and which, though to a certain extent highly necessary to our national prosperity, are, on the other hand, opposed to social and domestic happiness." A "counterpoise" to this "restless spirit of emigration" seemed to be manifest in the *"love of home"* evident in the rural estates of the Hudson River Valley (fig. 3).[7] These estates, as well as more modest rural and suburban homes, provided an atmosphere of rootedness. By the late 1840s Downing emphasized (through public parks) the importance of landscape in the rapidly growing American metropolis. For his expanding professional practice he hired Calvert Vaux.

3. A. J. Downing
ESTATE AT HYDE PARK
(from *A Treatise*
on the Theory
and Practice of
Landscape Gardening,
6th ed., p. 29, fig. 1.). 1860
Bard College Library,
Annandale-on-Hudson, N.Y.

The social goal of community could be brought about by improving the functional quality of private and public spaces. Downing listed utility as the highest priority of design. His talent was evident in his recommendations for the organization of interior domestic space, as well as in his planning of exteriors for specific functions—for example, orchards for fruit growing, kitchen gardens for vegetables, and flower gardens for decoration. Although he never had an opportunity to plan a public park such as those he visited in England in 1850, Downing was aware that urban parks would have to provide recreational activities such as walking and picnicking, which were readily available on Hudson River estates (Chap.2, fig. 6). During his short lifetime he saw the expanded recreational use of the Hudson River Valley by city dwellers, reflected, for example, in the opening of large resort hotels (Chap. 2, fig.10). Increased use intensified the need to preserve nature as the picturesque.[8]

Functional uses had to be harmonious with principles of design: the "look" had to fit the site. Downing preferred houses constructed of local materials in order to highlight regional character. The art of the landscape gardener was to adapt the site to the needs of the family, utilizing through asymmetrical planning the best orientation to views, sun, light, and air. Outdoor living was enhanced by Downing's design of porches, terraces, walks, and roads. Special attention was given to views and to selecting plant material suitable to the region, "sentiment," and function. In all of this, Downing believed that he was championing a modern style of landscape gardening that corresponded to a modern art of his age, landscape painting. "If art be at all manifest," he wrote, "it should discover itself only, as in the admirable painted landscape, in the reproduction of nature in her choicest developments."[9]

Olmsted, the codesigner of Central Park, also understood landscape gardening as a fine art. Visiting England in 1850, he wrote:

> Probably there is no object of art that Americans of cultivated taste generally more long to see in Europe, than an English park. What artist, so noble, has often been my thought, as he, who with far-reaching conception of beauty and designing power, sketches the outline, writes the colours, and directs the shadows of a picture so great that Nature shall be employed upon it for generations, before the work he has arranged for her shall realize his intentions.[10]

The aesthetics of Central Park were more important than those of private estates, for it was a public space in a region where nature was rapidly disappearing. This point was well understood by the noted art and architecture critic Clarence Cook, who had been Downing's assistant. In the most complete description of Central Park ever published, Cook wrote: "The best architecture and, indeed, the best art of whatever kind, can never be fully appreciated or enjoyed by those who have no familiarity with nature. The Park is only a blessing and a means of education, in proportion as it gives an opportunity to men, women, and children to become unconsciously familiar with the large traits of earth and sky."[11]

To maintain home and park with respect to function, appearance, and comfort, Downing, like Olmsted and Vaux, was a staunch advocate of technology. Downing was very concerned with questions of health and sought to improve the home through new methods of ventilation. The variety of structures he planned in rural estates—icehouses, hotbeds, greenhouses—involved considerable mastery of technology. Similarly, Central Park utilized the most advanced technology. Particular attention was given to building the most sophisticated system of drives and walks ever constructed in America. Without such a safe and comfortable road system, the designers understood, drivers and pedestrians would shun all avoidable areas. Clarence Cook observed: "On the Park our people have had the advantage of seeing the whole operation of building these admirable roads, which have never thus far been ever approached in thoroughness of construction and fitness for their several purposes, on this side of the water, and, probably, have never been surpassed anywhere."[12]

Neither landscape gardening nor landscape architecture was conceived of in opposition to technology; indeed, the major planning and design achievement of landscape gardening in the first half of the century, in addition to private estates, was the "rural" cemetery. Several of the artists discussed in this exhibition—Samuel F. B. Morse and Asher B. Durand—chose to be buried in Greenwood Cemetery (fig. 4), a model of landscape

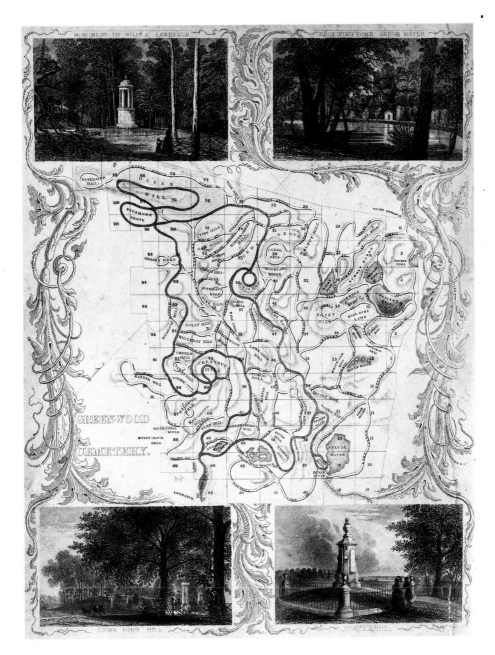

4. Map of Greenwood Cemetery (Frontispiece from *Green Wood*
by James Smillie, with descriptive notices by Nehemiah Cleaveland). 1847
Highly finished line engraving.
New York Public Library

art located near the then independent City of Brooklyn. The construction of such cemeteries was made possible by the knowledge and experience acquired in the building of canals, aqueducts, railroads, and rural estates; the aesthetic composition was influenced by the artist's perception of landscapes. It is no wonder that cemeteries became popular sites to visit while remaining private memorial spaces.[13]

While urban-oriented in many respects, such as location and views, rural cemeteries could not fulfill the growing social or cultural needs of large urban populations. In transforming landscape gardening into landscape architecture the planners were challenged to incorporate technology with minimal change in natural systems. The response can be seen in the work of such noted citizens of the region as Samuel F. B. Morse, such governmental leaders as DeWitt Clinton, and such cultural figures as the poet-publisher William Cullen Bryant, Downing's friend, who championed the planning of the nation's pioneer landscape architects, Olmsted and Vaux.

Samuel F. B. Morse: Artist-Inventor

Landscape gardening was regarded as an art form by the cultural leaders of the period. In a remarkable series of lectures at the New York Atheneum in March 1826, Samuel F. B. Morse classified the fine arts in terms of their aesthetic properties, "their principal aim [being] to please the imagination." Of the six arts that he considered "to be fine—as opposed to useful, necessary, or elegant—arts," only three were "perfect": poetry, music, and landscape gardening.[14]

Morse's definition of landscape gardening as a fine art is important for several reasons. He shows the continued attachment of Americans of his social background to English landscape design of the eighteenth century. There is a marked resemblance to Thomas Jefferson's understanding of landscape, for Morse—like Jefferson—cites a principal English authority, Thomas Whateley, in *Observations of Modern Gardening* (1770). As Morse's lectures make clear, he was familiar with the cultural and intellectual context of English eighteenth-century design—its relationship to democratic expression. An ambitious and talented young artist, Morse had lived in London from 1811 to 1815. One can assume that as a Jeffersonian democrat he was aware of the ideological contrast between English picturesque design and the aesthetics of French royal gardens such as Versailles.[15]

Morse's lectures also reveal his understanding of landscape gardening—indeed, of all the arts—as reflecting some divine aspect; for Morse, God was present not only in nature but in man's effort to work with natural materials. "An unperverted taste," Morse said, "must discern traces of the Deity in every thing: not a leaf, or an insect but speaks the language 'the hand that made me is divine.' " At the same time, Morse, like many of his contemporaries, believed that "man being mentally formed in the image of his Creator, possesses among other resemblances the desire and faculties of contriving with design."[16]

There is no indication in these lectures—or in anything else Morse wrote or thought during his long productive life—that he was at all concerned with the impact of technology on nature. In 1847 he purchased a one-hundred-acre estate in the Hudson River Valley, two miles from Poughkeepsie. His attitudes about Locust Grove are revealed in a letter written to his brother:

> I am almost afraid to tell you of its beauties and advantages. It is just such a place as in England could not be purchased for double the number of pounds sterling. Its "capabilities," as the landscape gardeners would say, are unequalled. There is every variety of surface, plain, hill, dale, glens, running streams and fine forest, and every variety of different prospect; the Fishkill Mountains towards the south and the Catskills towards the north; the Hudson with its varieties of river craft, steamboats of all kinds, sloops, etc., constantly showing a varied scene.[17]

Close to the expanding "village" of Poughkeepsie, the estate—really a large ornamental farm—rested within what appeared to be a socially cohesive community. As Morse expressed it, "within a few miles around, approached by excellent roads," he found "a most delightful neighborhood." He looked forward to the coming of the Hudson River Railroad, then being constructed, predicting happily that it would "run at the foot of the grounds (probably) on the river, and bring New York within two hours of us. There is every facility for residences—good markets, churches, schools. Take it all in all I think it just the place *for us all*."[18]

It is not surprising that Morse saw technology as beneficial. In 1847 he was better known as the inventor of the telegraph than as the artist-founder of the National Academy of Design in 1826. He had experienced all of the major changes that had transformed the wilderness into a pastoral landscape reflecting the ideal of the period. At a banquet in his honor in 1868, his friend the popular author William Cullen Bryant (fig. 5), while not as sanguine as Morse about technology, could still speak admiringly—if somewhat ominously—about Morse's contribution. Bryant told a distinguished group of New Yorkers during a lavish banquet at Delmonico's that Morse "had taken portions of the great electric mass, which in its concentrated form becomes the thunder-

5. Samuel F. B. Morse
PORTRAIT OF WILLIAM CULLEN BRYANT. 1825.
Oil on canvas, 30 x 20⅞″
National Academy of Design, New York

bolt; he has drawn it into slender threads, and every one of these becomes in his hands an obedient messenger—a printer's devil, carrying with the speed of a sunbeam volumes of copy to the typesetter." In the same speech, Bryant stated that *"Our guest has annihilated both space and time in the transmission of intelligence"* (italics added).[19]

On this occasion, Morse reiterated that "Science and Art are not opposed." He reminded his audience that some artists of the past had also been scientists and inventors, including "Leonardo Da Vinci . . . and our own [Robert] Fulton . . . a painter, whose scientific studies resulted in steam navigation." Morse's career was frequently compared to that of Fulton. Born in 1791, Morse could recall the public's excitement over Fulton's first steamboat voyage up the Hudson in August 1807.[20] By the time Morse bought Locust Grove, in 1847, steamboating was a regular part of the river landscape, shown as often in folk art as in fine art, and influenced the development of such river communities as Nyack, Piermont, and Haverstraw.

DeWitt Clinton and Regional Development: The Erie Canal

Morse understood the function of art in living history. As a portrait artist, he consciously sought to meet and paint the leaders of his time, such as DeWitt Clinton (fig. 6), who more than any other person of his generation understood the unity between New York City and the larger region. The descendant of a patrician-democratic family, Clinton, like his political mentor Thomas Jefferson, was a "Renaissance person," interested in technology and natural science. He served as mayor of New York City (1803–1806, 1808–1809, 1811–1815) and as governor of New York State (1817–1822, 1825–1828). He urged and facilitated the building of the Erie Canal, initiated in 1817 and completed in 1825 at a cost of $8,000,000. (The project was financed by the state, and the investment was repaid from tax revenues within seven years.)[21]

Clinton supported governmental assistance to other canals that also dramatically affected the Hudson River Valley. The Champlain Canal had been opened in 1823, linking the Hudson River with Lake Champlain at Fort Edward, "bearing . . . the wealth of a large internal commerce, extending from New York and Albany to Canada." The Delaware and Hudson Canal, completed in 1829, brought anthracite coal from Pennsylvania to the Hudson River at Kingston. As reported by Morse's Poughkeepsie neighbor, the artist-historian Benson Lossing,

> Immense piers have been erected in the middle of the stream for the reception and forwarding of coal. Here, and in the vicinity, are the manufactories of cement, and also extensive quarries of flagstone—all of which, with the agricultural products of the adjacent country, giving freights to twenty steamboats and many sailing vessels. Lines of steamers run regularly from Rondout to Albany and New York, and intermediate places, and a steam ferry-boat connects the place with the Rhinebeck Station.[22]

6. John William Hill
ERIE CANAL. 1831
Watercolor on paper, 9½ x 13½"
New-York Historical Society

Not all were optimistic about such changes. William Cullen Bryant and his friends—painter Thomas Cole, novelists James Fenimore Cooper and Washington Irving—as well as French commentators Alexis de Tocqueville and Jacques G. Milbert, questioned technology's implications for the natural resources of the region and, implicitly, for the nation. The fact that Cole and Irving lived in the Valley in year-round homes they helped design reflects this commitment to pastoralism. In general, however, most people saw canals as benefiting commercial and regional development. The Erie Canal popularized the picturesque character of the Hudson River by facilitating travel to the Adirondacks and Niagara Falls.[23]

The canal brought about large-scale economic and social changes within the region, but these were much less the result of physical intervention than of market forces responding to such changes. In fact, the planning, designing, and construction of the canal was done with consummate care and skill to minimize any impact on the land and attracted the sensitive response of landscape artists such as John W. Hill (fig. 7) and George Harvey.[24]

The canal was considered an outstanding example of what today could be termed landscape architectural engineering:

> A narrow ribbon of water 363 miles long, 40 feet wide at the top, and 4 feet deep was created between Albany and Lake Erie, with an additional twenty-two miles of canal connecting the Hudson River and Lake Champlain. In overcoming the 565 feet of elevation of Lake Erie over the Hudson at Albany, the Erie Canal followed a combined ascent and descent of 675 feet. The canal had eighty-three locks with lifts from six to twelve feet, and a succession of eighteen aqueducts which became the marvels of the day.[25]

7. Samuel F. B. Morse
DeWITT CLINTON. n.d.
Oil on canvas, 30 1/16 x 25 3/16"
The Metropolitan Museum of Art, New York. Rogers Fund

The Erie Canal gave enormous impetus to the economic growth of New York City as the major metropolis of the region and the nation: "The opening of the Erie Canal in 1825 . . . advanced the growth of New York City. . . . Period lithographs and watercolors invariably depict a lower valley jammed with sloops and steamboats. Commerce was brisk, most river towns flourished, and the lower valley was brought within the industrial and commercial sphere of New York City."[26] As Lossing wrote, the canal became Clinton's "enduring monument, whose bosom has borne sufficient food to appease the hunger of the whole earth, and poured millions of treasure into the coffers of the State."[27]

The Croton Water System

Clinton's regard for regional unity had led him to champion a farsighted development of New York City's water-supply system. In 1820, responding as governor to the menace of epidemic disease, he urged the state legislature to undertake a comprehensive plan for a pure water supply on which the city could rely for years to come: "A populous city like New York can never furnish, within its own limits, the resources of pure and wholesome water. Aqueducts conveying water from a distance have been used in all cities where the public health and the general comfort have been duly consulted."[28]

It would require the twin terrors, death by epidemic disease and destruction by fire, to force the issue. In 1832 Asiatic cholera struck the city, taking the lives of 3,500 persons and costing well in excess of $110,000. It was generally agreed that the absence of a pure water supply was a principal cause of the epidemic. In February 1833 a new state agency authorized Major David B. Douglass, a former army engineer and veteran of the War of 1812, to make a survey of water sources in Westchester County. Douglass's report endorsed the construction of a publicly funded aqueduct from the Croton watershed. His recommendation was accepted by the elected officials of the city, who were compelled by a state law of 1834 to submit the issue to a citywide referendum, held and passed on April 16, 1835.[29]

On December 16, 1835, before an analysis of the project had been presented, the city was devastated by one of the worst fires in its history. Twenty blocks of buildings burned down; two thousand businesses were forced into bankruptcy, including most of the insurance companies in the city; between five and eight thousand men and women were unemployed. A major cause of the devastation was an insufficient water supply to service the fire engines, dramatizing the need to hasten the completion of the Croton system.[30]

In 1842 the Croton waterworks was completed at a cost of some $13,000,000—a widely acclaimed public achievement in regional planning, design, and construction.[31] The dam was environmentally distinctive. Located some six miles north of the point where the Croton River enters the Hudson, solidly built of masonry, 270 feet long and fifty feet high, it held a lake five miles long, consisting of four hundred acres of water. The watershed or ridge line of the Croton Valley was 101 miles long. The Croton River was thirty-nine miles long, its tributaries 136 miles. The total area of the Valley was 352 miles, holding thirty-one lakes and ponds—a vast man-made landscape.[32]

As Lossing described it in his book on the Hudson River, the aqueduct provided a new aesthetic (fig. 8) that was an integral part of the river landscape:

> The Croton aqueduct runs parallel with the Hudson, at the mean distance of half a mile from it throughout its entire length. Its course is marked by culverts and arches of solid masonry, and its line may be observed at a distance by white stone towers, about fifteen feet in height, placed at intervals of a mile. These are ventilators of the aqueduct, some of them quite ornamental, as in the case of the one at Sing Sing, others are simple round towers, and every third one has a square base, with a door by which a person may enter the aqueduct. . . . Our little group shows the different forms of these towers, which present a feature in the landscape on the eastern shore of the river to voyagers on the Hudson.[33]

Indeed, the image of the Croton—representing purity, health, and cleanliness—was a powerful one within the city and the region for at least a generation. In 1855 the noted landscape painter and author Thomas Addison Richards, who was committed to the Hudson River Valley school of painting, included the Croton waterworks in an important travel book extolling the beauty of the American landscape. Covering the entire continent, he began his trip in New York with an illustration of the fountain sited in City Hall Park to celebrate the introduction of Croton water in 1842. The fountain (fig. 9) had to be understood, wrote Richards, in terms of "its great source, the immortal Croton."[34]

8. A. J. Downing
HIGH BRIDGE AQUEDUCT. c. 1861
New-York Historical Society

9. J. Addison Richards. THE PARK FOUNTAIN
(from *Romance of the American Landscape*, 1855, illustration no. II). 1853
Courtesy of Albert Fein

The Railroad, the Region, and the "Rural" Cemetery

While there is no evidence that Richards found the railroad inimical to the beauty of the American landscape, its impact disturbed others. In May 1846 the Hudson River Railroad was granted a state charter authorizing a grade-free steam railroad to run along the river from Canal Street to the tip of Manhattan Island. In December 1849 it was to be extended north to Poughkeepsie. By 1851 track had been laid as far north as Albany.[35] John B. Jervis, chief engineer for the railroad, responded to the complaints of landowners and others that the railroad "would destroy the natural beauty of the country as well as fail in its commercial object. On this point," he wrote, "I had claimed that the natural scenery would be improved; the shores washed by the river would be protected by the walls of the railway; and the trees, no longer undermined and thrown down by the river surf, would grow more beautiful; and that the railway thus combining works of art with those of nature would improve the scenery."[36]

Undoubtedly the railroad, more than any other mid-nineteenth-century development, shocked the sensibility of Americans, who placed greater value on solitude and on nature as wilderness. Yet it is reasonable to conclude that even such noted critics as Thomas Cole and Washington Irving came to appreciate the railroad's benefits.[37] Certainly it did not trouble Morse, who, like Jervis, saw it as perfectly harmonious with visions of the region. In 1851, with the railroad literally at the boundary of his Locust Grove home, Morse authorized the redesign of the house and the landscape after consulting the influential publications of Downing and Loudon. Morse, in short, not only did not worry about the railroad but viewed it as another technological wonder, enabling him to live a more complete life.

Morse's new summer home exemplified the picturesque aesthetic of the period. He employed Downing's close friend and collaborator, the architect-landscape gardener Andrew Jackson Davis, to help plan and design the house (cat. no. 23) as part of the landscape. Morse (Introduction, fig. 3) and Davis adhered to Downing's judgment that the most appropriate style for such a house was an adaptation of the Italian Renaissance-inspired villa, with emphasis on the garden. Morse was able to walk "from his study veranda toward the garden on paths edged with tulips, hyacinths, or fuchsias, discovering enticing vistas of lawn, field, river, and in the distance blue and green hills."[38]

Yet, as much as Morse loved his newly designed ornamental farm near Poughkeepsie, with its stables and greenhouses, he continued to spend autumn and winter in New York City in a brownstone on Twenty-second Street near Madison Square. He rejected the cemetery near his summer home as a final resting place for himself and his family: "Beautiful! Beautiful!" Morse declared in 1871, "but I shall not lie there. I have prepared a place elsewhere." The "place" was a plot in Greenwood Cemetery (fig. 10), near the City of Brooklyn.[39]

Morse's selection of Greenwood reflects his acceptance of landscape gardening's transition to regional landscape architecture. By the 1870s the "rural" cemetery was a well-established component of American cities. The locations of these cemeteries demonstrated the regional dimension of the emerging city; hence, in 1835, although Brooklyn was a newly designated independent municipality, Greenwood was also meant to serve New York City residents, anticipating the amalgamation of the two cities in 1898.

The "rural" cemetery in an urban setting also indicated the increasing secularization of American society, implicit in Morse's 1826 lectures. Physically separate from the church, the cemetery was part of the American urban landscape. In plan, design, and construction, these new spaces were antithetical to the crowded churchyards, which were understood to be sources of pestilential diseases.

The "rural" cemetery movement was international in origin. Its development can be traced to the influence of the English picturesque movement adapted in France in the eighteenth century. Introduced to the United States in 1831 with the establishment of Mt. Auburn Cemetery on the outskirts of Boston, the "rural" cemetery was soon adopted by most urban settlements in the country. The movement reflected new attitudes toward life and death, as well as toward art, architecture, and nature.[40]

10. Anonymous
SAMUEL F. B. MORSE MONUMENT
AND SITE IN GREENWOOD CEMETERY
Photograph
Greenwood Cemetery,
Brooklyn, N.Y.

11. Anonymous
DeWITT CLINTON MONUMENT
IN GREENWOOD CEMETERY
Photograph
Greenwood Cemetery,
Brooklyn, N.Y.

These cultural changes transformed the cemetery into a huge, quasi-public garden that became a popular place for walking and picnicking. Greenwood Cemetery, like Mt. Auburn and Poughkeepsie, was an adaptation of the picturesque imagery derived from the many estates being built in the vicinity of American cities,[41] the perceptions drawn by landscape painters, and the extensive technological information acquired through experience with steam energy, canals, aqueducts, and railroads.

"Rural" cemeteries were designed as permanent domestic landscapes resembling homes in the Valley in their respect for original topography, distant views, and native plant materials. Greenwood became the final resting place for many famous persons concerned with the regional landscape, such as DeWitt Clinton (fig. 11), artist John F. Kensett, and Asher B. Durand, landscape painting's most significant theorist.[42]

William Cullen Bryant, Andrew Jackson Downing, and the Movement for Central Park

William Cullen Bryant (1794–1878) and Andrew Jackson Downing were the two persons most responsible for the movement bridging landscape gardening and landscape architecture. Both believed that the impact of progress on the American landscape made government intervention essential. Just as government financed such interventions as canals and railroads, it must provide public spaces—"nature"—for growing cities and act to conserve the special places depicted by artists, such as Niagara Falls, the Adirondacks, and the Palisades.

Bryant was perhaps the most influential leader of New York City's cultural and social life during the nineteenth century. A founder of such art-oriented societies as the Sketch and the Century clubs, he was recognized in his day as one of the nation's most distinguished men of letters. His widely read Romantic poems "Thanatopsis" and "To a Waterfowl"—written before the age of twenty-one—made him the "poet laureate" of the American landscape. Durand immortalized this affinity with nature in his painting *Kindred Spirits* in 1849 (Introduction, fig. 1), locating Bryant and the artist Thomas Cole in Kaaterskill Clove, an area in the Catskills often visited by nineteenth-century artists.[43]

Bryant was the major speaker, as previously noted, at a banquet honoring Morse in 1868 and at the unveiling of a statue of him (fig. 12) in Central Park in 1871. The editor-poet located the thread connecting Morse's life as an artist to his career as an inventor—the movement toward systematization. Even as a painter, Bryant said, Morse "was strongly impelled to analyze the processes of his art, to give them a certain scientific precision, to reduce them to fixed rules, to refer effects to clearly defined causes, so as to put it in the power of the artist to produce them at pleasure and with certainty."[44]

This summation can also be considered critical of Morse, for systematization was the antithesis of the picturesque "nature" Bryant admired. It is not surprising that he saw the American landscape and democracy endangered—as Morse did not—by mindless territorial expansion and unrestricted technological advances. Bryant understood that the Hudson River Valley was a testing ground for the nation's destiny. His epic poem "The Ages" captures the sense of tension between "progress" and "nature" that prevailed throughout westward expansion. His concern with the fate of the landscape was most evident in his poem "An Indian at the Burial Place of His Fathers," written before 1832:

> But I behold a fearful sign,
> To which the white men's eyes are blind;
> Their race may vanish hence, like mine,
> And leave no trace behind,
> Save ruins o'er the region spread,
> And the white stones above the dead.[45]

Bryant was committed to active intervention. As owner and editor of the *New York Evening Post* and a major figure in the Democratic party, he was a significant social and political force. Under his leadership the *Post* became an influential advocate for a wide range of governmental interventions, including the Croton Aqueduct, new methods of fire and police protection, housing codes, and urban planning. Bryant was one of the first to recognize the importance of George P. Marsh's classic work on ecology, *Man and Nature* (1864), mentioning it in an 1865 editorial, "The Utility of Trees." Bryant argued forcefully that since Americans could not or would not voluntarily restrict the destruction of their forests, it was the duty of the government to intervene for the public good. In 1865 New York State, for example, successfully prohibited the plastering of advertisements on the rocks of the Hudson Highlands. Between 1872 and 1874 Bryant edited a major publication, *Picturesque America: or, The Land We Live In*, which included the engravings of many of America's foremost artists.[46]

Perhaps Bryant's most important public crusade took place in 1844, when he urged the construction of a large park in New York City. Traveling abroad regularly to study developments in Europe and elsewhere, he was impressed with the major changes in urban form in England, France, and Germany, resulting from new open spaces whose principal aesthetic was derived from nature. He believed that the city, as a primary source of civilized values, must be integrated with the countryside, even as each became a distinct region through technology. In New York, the economic and social capital of the nation, a large urban park designed according to aesthetic principles of landscape art and employing the highest standards of technology would constitute a new level of city and regional planning; such a concept would transform landscape gardening and invite a different description—landscape architecture.[47]

Bryant's crusade was supported by Andrew Jackson Downing, whom he met in 1847. This date marks Downing's ideological transition from conservatism devoted to private reform for middle- and upper-class people to a more democratic application of his knowledge of planning and design.[48]

12. Dam McPartlin/Parks Photo Archive
THE STATUE OF SAMUEL F. B. MORSE
IN CENTRAL PARK. 1962
Department of Parks and Recreation, New York City

Downing's transition was most evident in his attitude toward cities. At one time his home in Newburgh-on-the-Hudson had reflected an anti-urban feeling. His brother-in-law, Christopher Cranch, an artist and reformer, recalled that "when the gates of his villa closed it was a palace and garden all in one—all care and trouble were shut out, all joy and pleasure shut in." This attitude changed dramatically after Downing won international acclaim. His "society," recalled Frederick Law Olmsted, "was sought by the most successful men and women of the land and he was looked up to by these." Each of Downing's publications rapidly became a best-seller, for he captured the changing sensibility of the nation. Undoubtedly the books consulted by Morse in discussing the plan for Locust Grove with Alexander Jackson Davis were Downing's *Treatise on the Theory and Practice of Landscape Gardening, Adapted to North America* (1841), *Cottage Residences* (1842), and *The Architecture of Country Houses* (1850). Downing's major horticultural work, *The Fruits and Fruit Trees of America* (1845), was reissued fourteen times over a period of seven years.[49]

Downing became more concerned with urban issues by the 1840s when it had become apparent that the Hudson River Valley, including his home town of Newburgh, was being permanently transformed into a region with large urban concentrations housing many new immigrant groups. The nation confronted the challenge of integrating the foreign-born into the body politic, particularly its cities.[50] Downing saw landscape planning as a stabilizing force providing democratic places for education, socialization, and recreation. His successful magazine, *The Horticulturist*, found its major audience within the nation's largest cities and their suburbs.

13. John Bachmann. BIRD'S-EYE VIEW OF NEW YORK CITY SHOWING PARTS OF
WILLIAMSBURG AND BROOKLYN. 1850. Lithograph
New-York Historical Society

Downing had discovered a way to integrate his love and understanding of landscape gardening with a broader and more socially relevant realm of activity. He championed the application of landscape gardening for socially useful and public spaces such as "rural" cemeteries, planned suburbs, and, most important, urban parks. The technological developments of the region had made New York City at least as important to Newburgh as it was to the nation at large. Following Bryant's lead, Downing began urging the development of public parks for American cities in *The Horticulturist* of October 1848 and July 1849; his strongest editorials appeared in 1850 and 1851 while traveling in England. Comparing American urban development unfavorably with that of European nations, he wrote provocatively, "But the question may well be asked, is New-York really not rich enough, or is there not land enough in America, to give our citizens public parks of more than ten acres?"[51]

Downing died tragically in a riverboat accident in 1852. Had he lived, his capacity to cope with a project such as New York City's Central Park, begun in 1857, would have been complicated by the intense politicization of the overall process. While there were many reasons for public support of such a proposal, the legislative problems involved in designating parkland and authorizing funding were compounded by a struggle between city and state. The state legislature wished to see Central Park as part of the region that included other communities of the developing metropolis (fig. 13).

The state-revised New York City charter of 1857 established various commissions to handle municipal services in order to create a more rational administrative structure for interdependent communities—the beginning of regionalism. This was bitterly opposed by New York City's locally elected officials, such as Mayor Fernando Wood, as a violation of the rights of "home rule." It was under the Park Commission mandated by the state in 1857 that Olmsted was first appointed superintendent of construction and a year later successfully competed to design Central Park with Calvert Vaux.[52]

It was the intent of this commission and its designers to plan not only for a separate park (fig. 14) but for a metropolitan region whose physical form would be structured by parks and other open spaces such as parkways. This plan was not achieved in New York City, although it remained a basic concept at the end of the century, when landscape architects invented additional means for regional planning, including conservation of

14. John Bachmann
THE BIRD'S-EYE VIEW OF CENTRAL PARK, SUMMER. 1865
Museum of the City of New York. J. Clarence Davies Collection

wilderness areas, preservation of built landscapes, and designing of interstate parkway systems. The theory and practice of such planning reflected a concern with the aesthetics of nature central to painting.

A powerful American consensus about nature was reinforced by the writings of the English art and architectural theorist John Ruskin, who had attracted a following in this country in all design matters. The earliest American exposition of the aesthetic principles of nature as a source of art appeared in Asher B. Durand's "Letters on Landscape Painting," published serially during 1855 and 1856 in the pioneer design publication *The Crayon*. These ideas were shared by the founders of landscape architecture, who moved in the social and intellectual world of artists, particularly those devoted to the ideals of realistic landscape. Vaux (cat. no. 27), brother-in-law of the well-known painter Jervis McEntee (cat. no. 28), frequently accompanied McEntee and other artists on sketching trips through the Hudson River Valley. Unlike Vaux, Olmsted did not sketch or paint even as an amateur; however, through various professional experiences, including owning and editing *Putnam's Monthly Magazine*, an influential publication including discussions of art and architecture, he was familiar with many of the painters.[53]

The dominant concept expressed by Durand and shared equally by landscape painters and landscape architects was that a truly democratic, national aesthetic could not be developed by studying the landscapes of other countries or their depiction by indigenous artists; landscape art must be based on the "native resources" available to the painter. "Yes!" exclaimed Durand, "go first to Nature to learn to paint landscape [fig. 15], and when you shall have learned to imitate her, you may then study the pictures of great artists with benefit." Anticipating these sentiments, Bryant in 1829 penned a sonnet, "To Cole, the Painter, Departing for Europe":

> Thine eyes shall see the light of distant skies:
> Yet Cole! shall bear to Europe's strand
> A living image of our own bright land,
> Such as upon the glorious canvas lies.[54]

15. Asher B. Durand. LANDSCAPE: CREEK AND ROCKS. c. 1850
Oil on canvas, 16¹⁵/₁₆ x 24″
Pennsylvania Academy of the Fine Arts, Philadelphia. Gift of Charles Henry Hart

16. Charles H. Moore. LANDSCAPE: ROCKS AND WATER. c. 1860s
Watercolor and gouache over graphite on off-white paper, 7½ x 10¾″
Fogg Art Museum, Harvard University, Cambridge, Mass.

Central Park as Landscape Architecture

In a parallel way, landscape architects sought to amalgamate the indigenous qualities of a given site with images characterizing the American landscape—mountains and lakes, symbolized in rocks and water (fig. 16). In Central Park it was essential to preserve and accentuate the indigenous gneiss rock outcroppings (fig. 17), vestiges of a prehistoric age—God's working through nature—basic to the character of the site as well as symbolic of the larger American landscape. The rocky formation of Central Park, Calvert Vaux wrote, could not "compare favorably with the Kaatskills or the Adirondacks, but they are all the suggestion of the Kaatskills or the Adirondacks that thousands of our fellow-citizens will ever have an opportunity of studying; and for this, among many other reasons, we have treated them with particular respect from the outset."[55]

In the same way, all locations within the park that were depressed owing to geological processes would be considered logical outlets for lakes and ponds. Water should be sited in "natural basins" (fig. 18). It was important to adapt the images provided by lakes and streams located in American forests and wilderness areas painted by landscape artists. It is logical that Clarence Cook, as the author of an important book about Central Park, should have been a principal founder of *The New Path* (1863); the publication spoke for painters such as Thomas C. Farrer and Charles Moore, architects, geologists, and others who believed that "the proposed reform of American art was based upon principles of truth to nature and programs of study that were expounded by Ruskin."[56]

Cook wrote admiringly of the use of water within the park's wilderness section, the Ramble:

> A spring rises that feeds a slender stream which runs a short course till it falls into the Lake in its eastern division. This stream really drains what used to be a depression across the western half of the hillside on which the Ramble lies. It is no longer a marsh, but in one or two spots the ground is purposely left but partially drained in order that certain wild plants—reeds, lilies, irises, cardinal-flowers, and others that love such watery places, may have a home, and, not less, certain birds—storks, cranes, ducks, of the choicer and rarer sorts, pelicans, and herons.[57]

Another major component of the picturesque sensibility incorporated into Central Park was the concept of "the beautiful." This aesthetic, brought to an internationally recognized height of accomplishment in the lawns of English country estates and adapted for Hudson River Valley homes, was translated in Central Park to "a beautiful meadow in the centre of the park." Landscape architects, as much as landscape painters, were concerned with near, middle, and distant views. Aesthetics were also functional: picturesque composition was believed to inspire walking, riding, and looking. Nonetheless, the 820-acre park was not primarily an aesthetic object. Unlike painting—and much more than private landscape—Central Park was a year-round, multipurpose playground "whose open spaces [were] to be left for military parades, and large plats of turf for games, such as ball and croquet," and whose lakes were meant to encourage ice-skating and boating.[58]

Central Park was planned as part of the new city-to-be; nature was to be as integrated with the city as New York had become integrated with the region. The display of water within the park served to symbolize the city's dependence on water drawn from the Croton reservoir, as well as the utopian-based ideal of purity that governed urban planning in the middle of the nineteenth century. Central Park was often compared, in terms of urban achievement, to the completion of the Croton water system. It is understandable that the park should hold the city's first huge receiving reservoir of the Croton waterworks. By surrounding the reservoir with undeveloped parkland, the city was assuring New Yorkers of the continued purity of their water supply. In addition, the reservoirs would be connected by Morse's telegraph with police and fire headquarters; in the event of fire, even in times of drought, the authorities could increase the flow of water in specific sections of the metropolis.[59]

The park was to be open to all and visually welcoming. A low wall allowed views into it; the wide sidewalks surrounding it were meant to serve as tree-lined walks at night when the park could not be safely used; and the absence of gates and admission fees made it pervasively democratic. It was part of the city's planned rectangular form; the street system flowed into park openings and drives, and the transverse roads went from east to west below the park surface, allowing for unimpeded cross-town movement. The genius of designing three noncrossing traffic systems—for carriage, horseback rider, and pedestrian—was widely emulated.

17. G. W. Fasel
CENTRAL PARK ALBUM PLATE #VII: VIEW OF THE ENTRANCE OF THE CAVE AND STONEBRIDGE
Lithograph
Eno Collection, New York Public Library

18. G. W. Fasel
CENTRAL PARK ALBUM PLATE #5: VIEW OF THE LAKE LOOKING WEST
Lithograph
Eno Collection, New York Public Library

Great effort was made, as previously noted, to use the level of technology consonant with the function and aesthetic of the plan. This was evident in every aspect: waterworks, roads, drives, walks, bridges, arches, buildings, and, most of all, plant materials, many of which were grown in the park nursery. Olmsted wrote:

> I very much doubt if as many special problems came up requiring original engineering action or whether finer engineering skill was employed in all the enterprise of the Pacific Railroad as in the construction of Central Park. I doubt if all the street regulation and sewer, curbing, gutting and paving of the whole city of New York has called for such imaginary skill as has been used on the park.

As William Cullen Bryant expressed it: "Central Park is the pride of the metropolis."[60]

Pride of place was evident in every aspect of the design, which reflected a sense of power and optimism characteristic of the art and architecture of the period. In Central Park, as in the Hudson River Valley homes that artists such as Frederic Church, Albert Bierstadt, and Jasper Cropsey helped to design for themselves—respectively, Olana (cat. no. 34), Malkasten, and Aladdin (Chap. 4, fig. 4)—careful attention was given to siting that permitted viewing of and from the highest and most advantageous locations. As Cook noted:

> The visitor [to Central Park] must not be surprised to find his path leading by rocky steps and steep-up ascents to the north, until at length he finds himself on a bare summit that overlooks the lower Reservoir, and sees the whole lower park lying unrolled like a map at his feet. This point of rock is, we believe, the highest in the park, being one hundred and thirty-five feet above tidewater. . . . A structure called the Belvedere is in process of erection here, which is intended not merely to make a picturesque object seen from many points in the lower park, but to serve a useful purpose as well, being a spacious post for rest and observation.[61]

The Belvedere (fig. 19), however, was an exception to the architecture of the park in the same way that Olana, Malkasten, and Aladdin differed from the architecture of most of the homes and settlements built in the Hudson River Valley (see Chap. 4, fig. 13). Most of the houses depicted in this exhibition were more modest in scale and style and designed to identify with the region through use of native woods and stone. This was equally true in Central Park, where some of the structures meant for rest and/or viewing were built of local lumber in a distinctive design.

19. Olmsted, Vaux, & Co., Landscape Architects
DESIGN FOR THE BELVEDERE NORTH OF THE RAMBLE, CENTRAL PARK
Lithograph by Major & Knapp
Museum of the City of New York

20. Anonymous. RUSTIC ARBOR, CENTRAL PARK. n.d. Stereograph
Miriam and Ira D. Wallach Division of Art, Prints, and Photographs,
Astor, Lenox, and Tilden Foundations, New York Public Library

These functional, beautiful wood buildings (fig. 20) must have influenced the development of this art form nationally. As Cook wrote: "Hardly any thing of the sort had ever been seen before in this country. . . . The material employed is the common cedar, which so abounds in the vicinity of New York. The limbs and trunks are stripped of their bark, and . . . then put together in a solid and workmanlike fashion, very unlike the frail and flimsy structures that we commonly meet with under the name of summer-houses. Nor is it merely the workmanship that makes them noticeable, the design is always artistic and agreeable."[62]

Design details displayed a commitment to natural form popularized by the Hudson River Valley artists, who accepted technology but were concerned about the future of a nation in which commerce and industry were so rapidly changing the landscape. The care of the tree would symbolize the care of the landscape. Although there have been various interpretations of the significance of this first school of American landscape painters, their efforts can also be understood as an evocative documentation of scene and detail meant to enlighten future generations. This sense of the future pervaded the work of the landscape architects, who sought to introduce natural material in a growing metropolis. Only time would tell whether they had worked well and whether a modern urban society would maintain their principles. As Olmsted and Vaux wrote:

> Only twenty years ago, Union Square was "out of town"; twenty years hence, the town will have enclosed the Central Park. Let us consider, therefore, what will at that time be satisfactory, for it is then that the design will have to be really judged.
>
> No longer an open suburb, our ground will have around it a continuous high wall of brick, stone, and marble. The adjoining shores will be lined with commercial docks and warehouses; steamboat and ferry landings, railroad stations, hotels, theatres, factories, will be on all sides of it and above it; all which our park must be made to fit.[63]

As the park's designers understood, it is not possible to predict the future. It is, however, appropriate to note that the history of Hudson River art and of landscape architecture in the twentieth century reveals a powerful synergism based on decline and renaissance. That is to say, by the end of the nineteenth century the significance of the art of the landscape was largely lost on canvas as on the ground. In 1962 James Thomas Flexner, in the foreword to *That Wilder Image: The Paintings of America's Native School from Thomas Cole to Winslow Homer*, wrote:

> This will be the first modern work to deal fully with the Native Painting School as a whole. Many of the most significant painters have never been accorded full-length studies. Their pictures commonly languish in museum cellars or, if exhibited, have been allowed to remain so obscured with dirt that they can hardly be seen. Although no aspect of our artistic activity promises more fascinating insights into the nature and problems of American creativity, no important aspect of our culture has been less explored.[64]

It was not until the late 1960s that a serious effort was made to reinterpret the origins of landscape architecture; also at this time a significant body of literature on the life and work of Olmsted and the history of landscape architecture began to appear.[65]

The renaissance of interest in the history of both landscape art and landscape architecture is related on some level to a heightened awareness of the imbalance between technology and nature feared by nineteenth-century cultural leaders such as Cole, Bryant, and Irving. The harsh truth is that the natural spine of the region, the Hudson River, was dying, and that most important public expression of the Hudson River Valley aesthetic, Central Park, also appeared doomed, owing to poor management and social abuse. The emotions aroused by environmental issues gave particular poignancy to the rediscovery of artists concerned with nature.

In this context, the national environmental movement of the 1960s gained momentum when Con Edison sought to remove a part of the Storm King Mountain in 1963 in order to provide a site for a pumper-storage electric plant. An opposed coalition, the Scenic Hudson Preservation Conference, argued effectively for a more scientific understanding of the disastrous impact of continued technological abuse, while also furthering the application of technology to monitor and improve the quality of the river.[66]

The present was tied to the past. Basic to this regional effort, which established national standards, was a more complete appreciation of the past as set forth over a century ago by artists who had depicted the Valley. Storm King is typical of scenery popularized by leading painters of the nineteenth century. As one scholar has written with regard to the Scenic Hudson Preservation Conference, "implicit in the organization's title and in its use of nineteenth-century highland lithographs in its publicity brochures was the idea of 'Scenic Preservation'—saving land-forms that were beautiful today, still beautiful in fact because they were sanctified and mythologized in our romantic past."

Understandably, a leading historian of Hudson River Valley painters, John Howat, dedicated a major work on the subject to "Storm King Mountain and the Hudson Highland Gorge" and donated the royalties to the Scenic Hudson Preservation Conference.[67]

Threats to the viability of Central Park also provoked interest in its history and relationship to landscape architecture. In 1965 the park was designated New York City's first scenic landmark and was listed in the National Register of Historic Places. The following year Mayor John V. Lindsay, carrying out the campaign promise of his "White Paper on Parks and Recreation," appointed the first curator of Central Park, Henry Hope Reed. Although the title has changed, as well as the officeholder, there can be little doubt that the park has benefited from this recognition, which has fostered an appreciation of its history. Reed has noted approvingly the social and political opposition in the 1950s to diminishing the aesthetic and functional importance of natural elements by altering the park through building within it.[68]

It would be naive to believe that the renaissance of interest in the past coupled with concern for the present has resulted in the solution of all the problems of the Hudson River Valley or of Central Park. It is nonetheless reasonable to assume that this heightened awareness has motivated attempts to redress the worrisome imbalance between technology and nature. While no single factor within a complex social equation can protect such a regional environment, the historic record shows that in a democracy government responds best to those issues about which the public voices its concern most strongly.

The history of the Hudson River Valley is an example of how a nineteenth-century regional sensibility was forged through science and technology moderated by planning and design and profoundly affected by painters who cherished living there. This region, which includes a world capital, New York City, has witnessed how this sensibility reasserted itself more than a century later in defense and adaptation of the living history of river and park. It is fair to conclude, therefore, that the Hudson River region will continue to depend on a social amalgam in which artists and scientists have a leading role in maintaining the public's understanding of the quality of life. In the absence of such unity we cannot preserve the aesthetic and scientific integrity of the Hudson River Valley, of its regional manifestation in places like Central Park, and of the many communities it joins together; with such unity, there is optimism for the future.

1. Thomas Cole

LAKE WITH DEAD TREES. 1825

Oil on canvas, 27 x 34"

Allen Memorial Art Museum,

Oberlin College, Oberlin, Ohio. Gift of Charles F. Olney

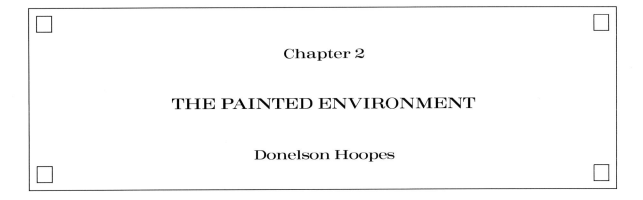

Chapter 2

THE PAINTED ENVIRONMENT

Donelson Hoopes

Despite its long history of colonial settlement, the Hudson River Valley was not a significant subject for artists until the early nineteenth century. Previous visual records of the region reveal a largely utilitarian purpose behind the creation of views that were the work of military artist-topographers.[1] Moreover, Pre-Romantic attitudes about the wilderness reveal an ambivalence that alternated between fascination with its splendor and repulsion provoked by the terror of its unknown power. Apprehensions of the sublime and terrifying aspects of nature pervade the writings of early travelers. Continental Army surgeon James Thacher, viewing the landscape in the highlands opposite West Point in 1778, recorded his observations of "hideous mountains and dreary forests, not a house in view. . . . Having reached the summit, we contemplated with amazement the sublime scene which opened to our view . . . huge mountains, rocky cliffs, and venerable forests in one confused mass."[2]

In the following decades, when New York changed from colony to state, the Hudson Valley became increasingly accessible, thanks to the introduction of steam navigation by Robert Fulton's *Clermont* in 1807. In 1825, with the opening of the Erie Canal, the river assumed a position of major importance as the connecting link between the port of New York and the developing western states. Travelers now eagerly embraced the picturesque beauty of the landscape, and their perceptions of nature reveal a profoundly altered attitude. Writing in 1832 about the same scene that had so perturbed Thacher, the English author Mrs. Frances Trollope saw only beauty:

> About forty miles from New York you enter upon the Highlands, as a series of mountains which then flank the river on both sides, are called. The beauty of this scenery can only be conceived when it is seen. One might fancy that these capricious masses, with all their countless varieties of light and shade, were thrown together to shew [sic] how passing lovely rocks, and woods, and water could be. Sometimes a lofty peak shoots suddenly up into the heavens, shewing in bold relief against the sky; and then a deep ravine sinks in solemn shadow, and draws the imagination into its leafy recesses. For several miles, the river appears to form a succession of lakes; you are often enclosed on all sides by rocks rising directly from the very edge of the stream, and then you turn a point, the river widens, and again woods, lawns and villages are reflected on its bosom.[3]

Mrs. Trollope's response to this landscape is literary and merely superficially descriptive. A more analytical understanding was expressed by her contemporary the Scottish novelist Thomas Hamilton, who saw in it the presence of a unique and harmonious ordering of nature:

> What struck me as chiefly admirable, was the proportion of the different features of the landscape. Taken separately, they were not much. Every one has seen finer rocks and loftier mountains, and greater magnificence of forest scenery, but the charm lay in the combination, in that exquisite harmony of detail which produces . . . a synthetic beauty of the highest order. Add elevation to the mountains, and the consequence of the river would be diminished. Increase the expanse of the river, and you impair the grandeur of the mountains. As it is there is perfect subordination of parts. . . .[1]

Against the backdrop of this felicitous gift of nature, American writers such as Washington Irving and James Fenimore Cooper elucidated the legends and history of the Hudson Valley in novels that stirred the popular imagination. Cooper's novel *The Pioneers* (1823), laden with descriptions of the Catskill Mountains, was published just as the area's foremost summer resort, the famed Catskill Mountain House, opened its doors to city-weary vacationers seeking the restorative benefits of nature. Coincidentally, the Romantic movement was emerging as the dominant force in the nation's art as the Hudson River Valley was about to become the incunabulum of the first school of American landscape painting.

Unlike his European counterpart, who was the product of social turmoil, disillusionment, international wars, and political reaction, the American Romantic artist reflected attitudes of optimism and hope based on a strong sense of harmony with his world. For many artists, the Hudson Valley offered the most accessible symbol of this integration and yielded abundant opportunities for pictorial expression. Moreover, they perceived the American wilderness as an uncorrupted state of creation, representing a higher moral order than was to be found elsewhere. The leading American art critic of the mid-nineteenth century, Henry T. Tuckerman, explaining the artists' new commitment to a metaphysical view of nature, wrote:

> Numerous modern artists are distinguished by a feeling for nature which has made landscape, instead of mere imitation, a vehicle of great moral impressions. . . . And where should this kind of painting advance if not in this country? . . . No blind adherence to authority here checks the hand or chills the heart of the artist. It is only requisite to possess the technical skill, to be versed in the alphabet of painting, and then under the inspiration of a genuine love of nature "to hold communion with her visible forms" in order to achieve signal triumphs in landscape, from the varied material so lavishly displayed in our mountains, rivers, lakes and forests—each possessing characteristic traits of beauty, and all cast in a grander mould and wearing a fresher aspect than in any other civilized land.[5]

Thomas Cole was one of the first artists to "hold communion" with the American wilderness. Perhaps because he grew up in the industrial English Midlands, Cole was quickest to respond to the idealistic notion of an unspoiled landscape. In 1825, six years after his arrival in the United States, he found his spiritual home in the Hudson Valley. The experience of his first visit to the Catskills remained indelible in his memory. In July 1836, on one of his frequent visits to the Catskill Mountain House, he recalled the mood of his first impressions that had been the genesis of *Lake with Dead Trees* (fig. 1),[6] painted eleven years before:

> We pursued our way to the lake. . . . I pointed out a view that I once painted; which picture, I believe, was the first ever painted of the lake that will be hereafter the subject of a thousand pencils. . . . I enriched my sketchbook with studies of the fine dead trees which stand like spectres on the shores. As we made our way through the woods . . . we perceived a rude boat among the bushes . . . we pushed it off. . . . Before us spread the virgin waters which the prow of the sketcher had never yet curled, enfolded by the green woods, whose venerable masses had never figured in the annuals, and overlooked by the stern mountain peaks, never beheld by Claude or Salvator, nor subjected to the canvas by the innumerable dabblers in paint of all past time. The painter of American scenery has, indeed, privileges superior to any other. All nature here is new to art. No Tivolis, Ternis, Mont Blancs, Plinlimmons, hackneyed and worn by the daily pencils of hundreds; but primeval forests, virgin lakes and waterfalls, feasting his eye with new delights, and filling his portfolio with their features of beauty and magnificence, hallowed to his soul by their freshness from the creation, for his own favored pencil.[7]

It was upon this kind of deification of nature that the American landscape tradition was founded. When Cole's lake subject was exhibited in 1825, it was among the group of pictures that first brought him to the attention of the leaders of the New York art establishment. The standard account of the meeting between the youthful Cole and these leaders, whose number included John Trumbull, was recorded by William Dunlap in his seminal work in the field of American art history.[8] From it, the reader is persuaded that Cole's pictures were greeted with admiration as well as some astonishment over their originality of conception. In point of execution they lacked academic finesse; yet that fact, rather than detracting, served to emphasize a certain intensity of feeling conveyed in the pictures. And however much Cole may have altered reality to fit his personal vision, his paintings had the effect of revealed truth. Cole's subsequent efforts continued to celebrate the sublimity of wild nature, attesting to an ever-increasing command of the medium and a marked sophistication in terms of composition. As he wrote to one of his first patrons, "Retired from the noise and bustle of N[ew] York and surrounded by the beauties of Nature, I shall have every opportunity of improvement I can wish."[9] While some of his major paintings, notably *Sunny Morning on the Hudson River* and *The Clove, Catskills*,[10] seem to be straightforward transcriptions of nature, there was already appearing in his work a new element that would assume a dominant role: the dialogue between man and nature.

For artists of the early nineteenth century, the American landscape presented a major defect in that, for the most part, it lacked historical associations and was regarded as mostly a raw topography. Having rendered this issue inapposite in the first of his Catskill Mountain pictures, Cole purposefully turned to incorporating

2. Thomas Cole
GELYNA. 1826
Oil on panel, 24 x 34½"
Fort Ticonderoga Museum, Fort Ticonderoga, N.Y.

notations of the human figure in the context of the wilderness, emphasizing the idea of the vulnerability of the former to the immensity and power of the latter. In a picture like *Gelyna* (fig. 2),[11] the two elements of historical association and human vincibility amid the vastness of nature are conjoined. The scene is no longer sunny and serene; tempestuous skies boil with angry clouds, threatening both man and landscape. It is painted as if Cole were assuming the mantle of Salvator Rosa in the New World. Symbolic and moralistic values began to take precedence over the naturalistic as Cole turned to what he called a "higher style of landscape." He began reach-

3. Thomas Cole
EXPULSION FROM THE GARDEN OF EDEN. 1827–28
Oil on canvas, 39 x 54"
Museum of Fine Arts, Boston. M. and M. Karolik Collection of American Paintings, 1815–1865

ing into his imagination for subjects that distanced his art from his own time and place, choosing biblical themes such as *Expulsion from the Garden of Eden* (fig. 3) and *St. John Preaching in the Wilderness*.[12] At the height of his career, Cole's predilection for the didactic reached its zenith in two suites of paintings dealing with themes of cosmic scope, "The Course of Empire" (fig. 4) and "The Voyage of Life" (fig. 5).[13] By investing his creative energies in this "higher style," Cole produced pictures that became sermons in paint. These proved ultimately disappointing to his contemporaries, who wished him to concentrate on painting American nature. Defending his position, Cole insisted it was the "duty" of the artist to dedicate himself to works that "enforce a moral or religious truth."

4. Thomas Cole. CONSUMMATION (from THE COURSE OF EMPIRE, a suite of five paintings). 1836
Oil on canvas, 51 x 76″
New-York Historical Society

5. Thomas Cole. YOUTH (from THE VOYAGE OF LIFE, a suite of four paintings). 1839–40
Oil on canvas, 52½ x 78½″
Museum of Art, Munson-Williams-Proctor Institute, Utica, N.Y.

6. Thomas Cole
THE PIC-NIC. 1846
Oil on canvas, 8½ x 13″
The Brooklyn Museum. A. Augustus Healy Fund, 1967.

Too much emphasis has perhaps been given to this side of Cole's art. During the last years of his life he produced some of the finest landscapes of his career, such as *The Pic-Nic* (fig. 6), which a friend called "a sylvan scene, all American, wide, bright, polished waters, manifold woods, over all the sweet glad light and quiet air, and every where the sense of beauty with wildness."[14] Through such paintings and his published writings on art for *The Knickerbocker* and other popular periodicals, Cole inspired a generation of painters.[15] In a lecture prepared for the National Academy of Design, Cole stressed his commitment to nature:

> Imitation is the means through which the essential truths of nature are conveyed. Thus art becomes the exponent of nature's highest qualities; she seizes the transitory forms of beauty; for truth and beauty (in their highest sense identical) are but the passing visitants and embodies them in permanent forms for our contemplation. . . . Through Nature we contemplate Art and Art discovers the beautiful in Nature—they are mutual exponents and the true student of Art must be a Student of Nature. . . .[16]

Cole believed that it was within the power of art to open the eyes of the viewer to the importance, even the necessity, of a spiritual relationship with nature. This conviction grew as each passing year brought new changes to the landscape in the name of material progress. From his home in Catskill he could see the majestic, undulating range of the nearby mountains, and one of his favorite diversions was to take walks along the Catskill Creek toward its source in those mountains. The area's first major industry, the tanning of animal hides, was

7. Thomas Cole
VIEW ON THE CATSKILL, EARLY AUTUMN. 1837
Oil on canvas, 39 x 63"
The Metropolitan Museum of Art, New York. Gift in Memory of Jonathan Sturges by his children, 1895

responsible for the initial depletion of the abundant stands of hemlocks that Cole greatly admired. This dese-cration moved him to compose a poem, giving vent to his feelings; the tenor of this 1834 sonnet, "On Seeing that a Favorite Tree of the Author's Had Been Cut Down," is decidedly Wordsworthian and was probably too artful to serve as the kind of polemic he undoubtedly intended it to be.[17] His most fully developed discourse on the subject of nature, "Essay on American Scenery," was published two years later and was aimed at the general public.[18] In it Cole urged his readers to look upon nature with a "loving eye":

> The delight in nature . . . a man experiences is not merely sensual, or selfish . . but in gazing
> on the pure creation of the Almighty, he feels a calm, religious tone steal through his mind,
> and when he has turned to mingle with his fellow men, the chords which have been struck in
> that sweet communion cease not to vibrate. In this age . . . what is sometimes called improve-
> ment, in its march makes us fear that the bright and tender flowers of the imagination shall all
> be crushed beneath its iron tramp. . . . The pleasures of the imagination, among which the love
> of scenery holds a conspicuous place, will alone temper the harshness of such a state. . . .

Ironically, Cole's idyllic refuge from the distractions of city life—his "rural nature" in Catskill—was tainted by encroaching industrial development from the moment he settled there permanently in 1836. In that year the Canajoharie and Catskill Rail Road began clearing its right of way along Catskill Creek at precisely the site of one of Cole's favorite rambles.[19] He fulminated about this frequently in letters to sympathetic friends like

Asher Durand and Luman Reed: "The copper-hearted barbarians are cutting *all* the trees down in the beautiful valley on which I have looked so often with a loving eye . . . tell this to Durand, not that I wish to give him pain; but that I want him to join with me in maledictions on all dollar-godded utilitarians."[20]

Despite his discontent with such depredations, Cole's mature paintings of his environment seek to express the theme of mankind's rewarding accommodation with nature domesticated, in keeping with his notions of the ideal "rural" landscape. In *View on the Catskill, Early Autumn* (fig. 7),[21] he eliminated the offending presence of the railroad; the emphasis here is the dream of an ideal pastoral perfection in which man and nature coexist in harmony. As he saw it, the artist's mission was to amplify the "heart-touching associations" that the ordinary man experienced in the presence of nature, and so improve the human spirit. This optimism was expressed in a lecture he delivered to his Catskill neighbors in 1841:

> The Hudson, for natural magnificence is unsurpassed. What can be more beautiful than the lake-like expanses of Tapaan [sic] and Haverstraw as seen from the rich orchards of the surrounding hills? What can be more imposing than the precipitous Highlands, whose dark foundations have been rent to make a passage for the mighty river? The lofty Catskills stand afar off; [and] recede like steps by which we may ascend to a great temple. . . . The Rhine has its castled crags [but] the Hudson has its wooded mountains . . . and an unbounded capacity for improvement by art.[22]

This "unbounded capacity," as demonstrated by Cole, became the foundation for the first truly indigenous school of American painting. The Hudson Valley's "harmony of detail which produces . . . a synthetic beauty of the highest order," as noted by Thomas Hamilton, was seized upon by a growing corps of American landscape painters who, after Cole's untimely death in 1848, were led by Asher B. Durand. Although he was Cole's senior, Durand did not turn to painting until the 1830s, well after he had established a reputation as one of the nation's foremost engravers. Portrait and genre painting earned him a livelihood, but Durand's principal desire was to excel as a landscape painter, and Cole served as his early model. As he wrote to Cole:

> I am still willing to confess myself a trespasser on your ground, though, I trust, not a poacher; landscape still occupies my attention. . . . Now if there be a man on earth whose location together with whose locomotive powers I envy, it is Thomas Cole! . . . were I so circumstanced . . . the vast range of this beautiful creation should be my dwelling place [but] the only portion . . . I can at present avail myself [is] the neighborhood of Hoboken. . . .[23]

Confined to the city for most of the year, Durand made the most of his summer painting trips, ranging from the Catskills to the Adirondacks, the White Mountains, and the Berkshire hills of western Massachusetts—travels that took him, as his son wrote, to "every nook and corner and 'clove.'" By the late 1840s he began concentrating on the Catskills to the extent that, largely through his proselytizing, the village of Palenville at the southern end of Kaaterskill Clove became the area's first art colony. Here such artists as David Johnson, John F. Kensett, Christopher P. Cranch, and John W. Casilear were joined by writers in discussions of the aesthetic virtues of the Catskill scenery.

In his own painting Durand favored specificity in the depiction of individual tree forms, such as in *Landscape with Birches*,[24] although he tended to carry on some of Cole's elements of pictorial design, such as the use of trees as framing devices for vistas. But under Durand's tutelage the younger artists began to be led away from the moralizing aspects of Cole's art toward a more straightforward realism, based upon a close observation of nature. Indeed, Durand's transcending contribution to the progress of American art may be seen in his work as a theorist. The essence of his artistic principles was clear and direct:

> Let me earnestly recommend . . . one studio which you may freely enter and receive in liberal measure the most sure and safe instruction . . . the Studio of Nature.[25]
>
> Take pencil and paper [first] and draw with scrupulous fidelity . . . productions . . . imbued with that indefinable quality recognized as sentiment or expression which distinguishes the true landscape from the more sensual and *striking* picture.[26]

In his own painting Durand favored a style that often involved a tactile surface treatment; yet his advice to students warned against dependence on this practice: "The greatest achievement in the producing of fine color is the concealment of pigments, and not the parade of them; and we may say the same of execution. The less apparent the means and manner of the artist, the more directly will his work appeal to the understanding and the feeling."[27] By this injunction Durand pointed the way for the younger generation of artists such as Gifford and Church and the development of that aspect of American landscape painting known as Luminism.

8. Frederic E. Church
TWILIGHT IN THE WILDERNESS. 1860
Oil on canvas, 40 x 64″
Cleveland Museum of Art.
Mr. and Mrs. William H. Marlatt Fund

The artist who would become the prime exponent of Luminism, Frederic Edwin Church, found his perfect mentor in Cole, the master of the heroic landscape. As Church expressed it when he was accepted as Cole's student, "My highest ambition lies in excelling in the art. I pursue it not as a source of gain or merely as amusement."[28] Church proved himself an apt pupil who possessed, as Cole said, "the finest eye for drawing in the world." Two years after he began his studies with Cole, Church was sufficiently advanced to have his first major landscape included in the spring exhibition of the National Academy of Design. Significantly, this picture blended landscape painting with historical narrative in a kind of reprise of Cole's own modest youthful efforts like *Gelyna*.[29] While Church's early work includes biblical subjects and reflects Cole's preoccupation with such themes, Church responded to calls from his contemporaries to "know and feel with [this] age" and to turn away from the past.

Church rejected Cole's essentially anthropomorphic view of nature, with its attendant autobiographical ruminations, in favor of a confrontation with the actualities of the landscape. In *Twilight in the Wilderness* (fig. 8),[30] he broke through the essentially Claudian structures of landscape painting as preached by both Cole and Durand. In the words of Church's biographer, "Out of nature experienced and art re-created, he produced the very picture of his time and place. It was original. It was radically new. It was America as the Second Beginning."[31]

9. Sanford R. Gifford
HUNTER MOUNTAIN, TWILIGHT. 1866
Oil on canvas, 30½ x 54″
Terra Museum of American Art, Chicago. Daniel J. Terra Collection

The same year he completed *Wilderness* Church began acquiring property near Hudson, New York, directly across the river from Cole's house at Catskill, where his journey as an artist had begun. Traveling the world from the Andes of Ecuador to the frozen seas off Labrador and to the cradle of civilization in the Near East, Church projected himself as an artist in much the same spirit of discovery as Cole, in his more circumscribed way, had ventured into the American forest. That Church chose a site for his elaborate house, Olana, at a place not only overlooking the Catskills and the Hudson River but also the property of his honored teacher was emblematic of his acknowledgment of his origins as an artist. Olana, the "center of the world," as he called it, became Church's ultimate work of art, one in three dimensions rather than two. As he expressed it, "I can make more and better landscapes in this way than by tampering with canvas and paint in the Studio."[32]

If Church's contribution to American art was to revise Cole's historicism to embrace a broader view of nature's cosmic process, Sanford Gifford's achievement was to incorporate this view within the context of traditional Hudson River School subject matter and mood. No less a world traveler than Church, he noted: "The harm which sometimes happens to American painters from too long a sojourn in Europe . . . arises, I think, from subjecting oneself too long to the influence of a particular school of painting."[33]

Growing up in the town of Hudson, New York, Gifford, more than any other American artist of his time, was in the closest physical proximity, not only with Cole (for whose works he felt the "greatest admiration") but also with the heartland of American landscape painting, the Catskill Mountains. He probably shared his contemporaries' opinion that Cole had embraced too closely Old World models in the area of allegorical painting, but Gifford's earliest productions, such as *A Scene in Northern New York*,[34] acknowledge a debt to Cole's poetic transcriptions of nature. Believing that no historical associations that might obtain to the scenes that attracted him could be of any possible use to the landscape painter, Gifford concentrated on the sublimity of atmospheric phenomena. In the most successfully realized paintings of his mature years, such as *Kauterskill Clove*,[35] he subordinated naturalistic detail to the subtle effects of colored light. In his pursuit of the transient moment between sunset and dusk, as seen in *Hunter Mountain, Twilight* (fig. 9),[36] Gifford stands as the quintessential Luminist painter, for whom "landscape-painting is air-painting."[37]

10. Jasper F. Cropsey
CATSKILL MOUNTAIN HOUSE. 1855
Oil on canvas, 29 x 44"
Minneapolis Institute of Arts. William Hood Dunwoody Fund

As one of the most accomplished draftsmen of the Hudson River School, Jasper Cropsey adhered to Durand's injunctions to the artist to be scrupulous in the study of nature "as she is":

> This mode of study is productive of knowledge—it makes a man a botanist, a geologist, he is not satisfied in seeing things merely upon the surface. He studies deeper. The knowledge he gains is communicated to his work, so that while it possesses beauty as a work of art, it is scientific and historical—scientific from the great character that pervades it, and historical because of the truthfulness with which it represents the country. . . .[38]

At the time Cropsey wrote this, indigenous naturalist tendencies in American art were finding a strong theoretical support on the international scene. Under the leadership of the English critic and writer John Ruskin, who published the first volume of his influential *Modern Painters* in 1843, artists on both sides of the Atlantic responded to his call for a "faithful and loving representation of nature." Even so, Cropsey was not immune to the strong Romantic force of Cole's art, in terms of both subject matter and technique. This is amply demonstrated in *Storm in the Wilderness*,[39] a scene depicting Kaaterskill Clove caught in a mood of nature which Cropsey described as "furious." A few years later, painting the more serene *Catskill Mountain House* (fig. 10),[40] he chose the identical prospect used by Cole when he painted this subject,[41] but Cropsey's treatment incorporated a freedom of touch with an exactness in rendering the components of the landscape that marked a distinct advance beyond Cole's idealized concept of nature. One is particularly struck by the luminous clarity of the sky in Cropsey's picture, which stands as a prototype for the kind of Luminist painting that would flourish in the next decade. Cropsey enunciated the terms of the Luminist aesthetic in an essay he wrote for *The Crayon*: "Of all the gifts of the Creator—few are more beautiful, and less heeded than the sky. . . . Here we have first the canopy of blue; not opaque, hard and flat, as many artists conceive it and picture patrons accept it, but a luminous, palpitating air, in which the eye can penetrate infinitely deep and yet find depth."[42]

Cropsey never pursued Luminism to its logical extreme, however, as Gifford did. For Cropsey, nature had to be closely observed in all its varied manifestations; and in the work of his middle years there is always a

11. Albert Bierstadt
DOMES OF YOSEMITE. 1867
Oil on canvas, 116 x 180"
St. Johnsbury Athenaeum, St. Johnsbury, Vt.

feeling for the particular place in his landscapes. At the first public presentation of his masterpiece, *Autumn on the Hudson*,[43] Cropsey was careful to provide a printed leaflet pointing out the identity of the places represented. This painting is a treatment of the native scene on the same scale as Church's seeking to reveal the wonders of nature in South America. And, like Church, Cropsey's venue evolved from the ethic of nature as the manifestation of a divine spirit. As such, their works were elaborations on the principle of the underlying moral values in art—their legacy from Thomas Cole. However, their paintings also intimate the future, as symbols of America's manifest destiny, which would find ultimate expression in the art of Albert Bierstadt.

While Cropsey's autumnal visions of pastoral nature remained fixed in the mainstream tradition of the Hudson River School, with its reliance upon the faithful study of nature, Bierstadt's monumental Western panoramas proclaim no such concern. His use of the camera substituted for sketching more often than not, and he sought to intensify the impact of nature through exaggerations of scale and dramatic effect that were unthinkable to most School men. Bierstadt's ascendancy coincided with Church's decline through illness in the late 1870s. For Bierstadt, this was fortuitous, in the sense that Church was his only serious rival in the field of large-scale landscape painting. His first encounter with the grandeur of the Western landscape came in 1859 as a member of an Army surveying expedition charged with mapping an overland route from Saint Louis to the Pacific. In a letter to *The Crayon* he expressed an interest in nature that seems to echo Cropsey's injunction that an artist should be "a botanist, a geologist":

> The [Rocky] mountains are very fine . . . of a granite formation . . . the lower hills [are] clothed with a great variety of trees . . . cottonwood lining the river banks, the aspen, and several species of fir and the pine . . . . We see many spots in the scenery that remind us of our New Hampshire and Catskill Hills, but when we look up and measure the mighty perpendicular cliffs that rise hundreds of feet aloft, all capped with snow, we then realize that we are among a different class of mountains.[44]

Upon his return to the east, Bierstadt settled in New York City, where he exhibited the first of his spectacular western landscapes, *Storm in the Rocky Mountains*.[45] By 1865 his national reputation was assured, and his paintings were commanding the highest prices ever paid to that date for the work of an American artist, surpassing even Church. Both were successful, worldly gentlemen-artists, far removed in manner and style from men like Cole and Durand, whose modest mien precluded ostentatious living. Bierstadt's thirty-two-room villa and studio at Irvington-on-Hudson was as much the scene of a glittering social round as it was the place where the artist executed his most grandiose paintings, such as the wall-sized *Domes of Yosemite* (fig. 11).[46]

On occasion Bierstadt turned his creative eye upon his immediate surroundings and produced works of undeniable charm. These pictures are departures from his usual style; in them one finds a mood of quiet contemplation and a feeling for "that exquisite harmony of detail" that are the heart of all Hudson River School painting. Absent are the distortions of reality that in his Western landscapes turn nature into a kind of painted grand opera; yet it is precisely in the latter vein that Bierstadt laid his claim to distinction. In 1889, one of his most histrionic western subjects[47] was rejected by a jury of his peers who were selecting paintings for the American section of the Paris Exposition; Bierstadt was deemed no longer interesting. By the late nineteenth century, fashions in art were being dictated by standards of taste imported from France.

12. George Inness
THE LACKAWANNA VALLEY. 1855
Oil on canvas, 33⅞ x 50¼"
National Gallery of Art, Washington, D.C. Gift of Mrs. Huddleston Rogers, 1945

Of the many American painters who were deeply influenced by French art, and in turn stimulated an interest in it, George Inness was singularly successful in creating his own style, which he freely adapted from his study of the Barbizon School. His early landscapes, however, reflect the influence of the Hudson River School, particularly the work of Durand. But Inness quickly discarded traditional compositional format and philosophy. *The Lackawanna Valley* (fig. 12)[48] partakes of a certain colorful luminosity of atmosphere in the manner of Gifford; yet its subject, the celebration of the impact of civilization upon nature, marks a radical departure from Cole's ideal of the pastoral "rural landscape." Inness frankly acknowledged modern progress in his art, preferring a "civilized landscape," as he termed it—one that favored evidence of man's intervention in nature over scenes of untouched wilderness:

> The highest art is where has been most perfectly breathed the sentiment of humanity. . . . Some persons suppose that landscape has no power of communicating human sentiment. But this is a great mistake. The civilized landscape peculiarly can; and therefore I love it more and think it more worthy of reproduction than that which is savage and untamed. It is more significant. Every act of man, every thing of labor, effort, suffering, want, anxiety, necessity, love, marks itself wherever it has been.[49]

Over a period of two decades Inness developed his highly individual style of painting, turning from conventional representations of nature toward broader, tonal statements distinguished by glowing color. By the 1880s he had synthesized form and color into an intensely poetic vision of the "civilized landscape." It was at this stage in his career that he "became very enthusiastic about figure-painting and decided to go into that almost to the exclusion of the broader subject."[50] Circumstances led Inness to embark upon this new interest at Milton, New York, in the Hudson Valley during the summer of 1881. There he combined the "broader subject" of the well-ordered countryside with representations of the local residents who, he said, "make capital models." Well pleased with what he accomplished at Milton, he noted that one picture in particular "seems to express grandeur better than anything I have done."[51]

In contemplating the paintings of Inness's mature years, one senses a fusion of influences at work, notably the Barbizon School and Impressionism. Nevertheless, these remain subservient to his individual vision as an artist. In particular, Inness rejected the notion that he was a disciple of the latter:

> Long before I ever heard of impressionism, I had settled in my mind the underlying law of what may properly be called an impression of nature, and I felt satisfied that whatever is painted truly according to any idea of unity, will as it is perfectly done possess both the subjective sentiment—the poetry of nature—and the objective fact sufficiently to give the commonest mind a feeling of satisfaction.[52]

Inness very rarely sketched out of doors, preferring to work in the studio, where his paintings evolved from recollections of nature. It is this approach that gives his paintings their dreamlike quality and constitutes the culmination of the long search in American art for the ideal landscape. With Inness, it is possible to see the closing of a vast creative circle that began with Cole. There are striking parallels between the two artists in their convictions about the essentially spiritual significance of nature and man's relationship to that nature—and even between the methods by which they consummated a work of art. As Cole wrote to Durand, "Have you not found?—I have—that I never succeed in painting scenes, however beautiful, immediately on returning from them. I must wait for time to draw a veil over the common details, the unessential parts, which shall leave the great features . . . dominant in the mind."[53]

The Hudson Valley continued to play a role, albeit a diminished one, in the progress of American art into the early twentieth century. Especially from the west bank inland, around and in the Catskills, artists still found invigorating environments in remote mountain villages such as Arkville or in the more elegant precincts of Onteora Park. When Cole first ventured into the Catskills, the area was a three-thousand-square-mile tract of wilderness; the changes that occurred there in his lifetime and afterward altered this condition but did not destroy it. As the historian Roland Van Zandt observed, discussing the aftermath of the first inroads of settle-

13. Anonymous
VIEW OF MINK HOLLOW FROM NEAR BECKWITH'S HOUSE
From an album of views entitled *Onteora Photographs to Order.* n.d.
Silver gelatin photograph, sheet, 10⅛ x 13¼"
Courtesy of Onteora Club, N.Y.

ment, "The Catskills always remained a characteristic fusion of the wild and the domesticated, of smooth lawns and formal drives in the midst of unkempt forests and rushing mountain streams, but by the end of the [nineteenth] century they were never less a wilderness, never more a humanly contrived landscape."[54]

Within a century, what had been terrifying, "hideous mountains and dreary forests" in the eyes of eighteenth-century travelers was converted to "civilized landscape" through the work of writers, architects, landscape designers, and, most significantly for the nation's cultural heritage, the vision of its artists.

1. Anonymous
BECKWITH AND FRIENDS ON A PORCH AT ONTEORA PARK
(The second man from the right is Brander Matthews;
Beckwith is at the extreme left). c. 1892
Silver gelatin photograph, 5¾ x 7⅜″
Courtesy of Onteora Club, N.Y.

During the long-ago summers these landscape painters went their several ways. . . . When Autumn was at its height of color and beauty there was generally a convocation for a week or two at some place in the Catskills where scarlets and crimsons, and orange and gold contrasted with the blue mists of airy distances and cloudy skies, and where the days were spent in walking, sketching and pure enjoyment. Some of the most enjoyable days of my life were passed in this companionship. Cole was still living at Catskill, and painting in the mountains. George Hall had built a small house on the Kaaterskill Clove which was an occasional stopping place on a long day's tramp. Gifford's family home was at Hudson in sight of all the majesty of the mountains. McEntee's country home and studio were at Rondout. Church had built a beautiful house in the middle of an estate some miles below, and in sight of the river, and here he spent the summers after his wandering and bachelor days were over, fitting into this ideal country home bits of beauty from all lands and places. The Hudson and the Catskills were dear to all these men, and from them they derived inspiration and happiness.[1]

Chapter 3

DOCUMENTS OF THE PERSONAL LANDSCAPE

Sandra S. Phillips

I n 1855, Asher B. Durand wrote that the artist should go to nature "with veneration,—and find in the conscientious study of her beauties all the great first principles of Art." After Thomas Cole's premature death in 1848, Durand's modest personality, coupled with his sure vision of nature, caused him to become the focal member of the group of landscape painters we call the Hudson River School. Like his contemporaries Church and Bierstadt, he was interested in depicting the actuality of nature, idealized but eminently material. At the time he wrote his notes in *The Crayon*, he was making direct studies from nature to be used in his large compositions painted during the winter months.[2] Durand's work is a clear example of the dual attitude to nature found in the Hudson River artists: the marriage of a sense of real, material place with an ideal, most wonderfully realized in *Kindred Spirits*.

Though Durand purchased a home south of Newburgh in 1849 and appears to have spent at least two summers there, he is one of the few artists considered in this study who apparently had little interest in his immediate environment. He seems to have used his house more as a way station to the wilderness than as a place he documented or personally modified. Most of the artists who settled in this general region did modify their personal environments and documented them often in paintings, drawings, or photographs. The houses in which they lived, the studios where they worked, even the vistas from their homes, were extensions of their art. Thus common reality extended to embrace an ideal.

A sense of the aesthetic home, of personal and specific place evoked by these images, is interesting to us not only because these houses and studios belonged to Hudson River artists, some of them of considerable stature, but because there is such obvious care, warmth, and curiosity in many of these images. For artists with a real interest in photography, documenting their home or workplace was a natural expression. An interest in landscape and architectural design, and often the recording of it, was related to an interest in forms of visual documentation or pictorial expression considered marginal today or outside the usual parameters of fine art.

Many artists were essentially depictors of topographic views. They used, or were at least familiar with, the great variety of drawing aids available to nineteenth-century artists—the camera obscura, the camera lucida, and their variants, which included a lens that would throw the view in question onto a flat surface, more or less easily traced by the artist. Some painters were fascinated by the panorama, a popular form of entertainment something like a film travelogue. Panoramas were often long paintings, gradually unfurled on rollers, sometimes with musical accompaniment and a speaker pointing out the sights. The most famous was John Banvard's *Mississippi River Panorama*, although William Dunlap, an artist most famous for his early history of American art, executed a panoramic moving backdrop of Hudson River views for his play, *A Trip to Niagara*. The Kingston artist John Vanderlyn was a painter of the still panorama on a circular wall, intended to give an optically correct and overall view of a scene. Other artists were interested in stereoscopy or lantern slides, which were often colored and used in lectures. All these marginal visual forms respected a sense of the exactitude of the place depicted and often an idealization of it at the same time.[3]

The first Hudson Valley artists who took an interest in their personal environment were essentially topographers. George Harvey was a painter of views, intended for some form of reproduction, either in aquatint or as lantern slides. An Englishman who arrived in this country in 1820 and settled along the Hudson at Hastings, he earned a reputation as a miniaturist but became so exhausted from the practice of this demanding art that he gave it up. He bought land at Hastings in 1834 and designed and built his house and grounds as a restorative.

> A country life and exercise being recommended, he purchased a tract of land on the majestic Hudson River—built a cottage after his own plan—amused himself in laying out the grounds—and thus gained health and strength by the employment. These exercises in the open air led him particularly to study and notice the ever-varying atmospheric effects of the American climate. He undertook to illustrate them with his pencil, and thus, almost accidentally, commenced a set of atmospheric landscapes.[1]

He titled one of these watercolors, probably his own home, *An Elizabethan Cottage on the Hudson*, but town residents referred to it as The Castle. The main structure and some of the outbuildings were built with marble from the quarry on his own lot.

Harvey was most sensitive to the scenery of the Hudson, to its civilized aspect rather than its wildness, as well as the particular sense of light and airiness he was able to capture with his miniaturist's technique. He helped Washington Irving redesign Sunnyside nearby and then painted it. Harvey's atmospheric delicacy and sense of concrete actuality are evident in *Afternoon—Hastings Landing, Palisades, Rocks in Shadow, N.Y.*, c. 1836 (cat. no. 2), which was painted not far from his house (the Hudson was called the North River at that time). The next year he went to England in an attempt to have his watercolor views engraved but was unsuccessful. Harvey is known to have supported himself in England by lecturing on American scenery illustrated with hand-tinted lantern slides made from his watercolors. He returned to America and in 1847 was forced to sell his property at Hastings in order to raise money to have his pictures engraved, although only a few of them ever were.[5] Two years later the Hudson River Railroad cut through the Harvey property.

A group of Hudson River artists committed to depicting topographical views was the Hill family of Nyack. The eldest, John Hill, bought property to build a home on the Nyack Turnpike in 1836. He was an established master of aquatint and engraving before emigrating from England in 1816. Hill was contracted to execute the prints for Joshua Shaw's *Picturesque Views of American Scenery* in 1819 and the reproductions of William Guy Wall's watercolors in the *Hudson River Portfolio*, beginning in 1821. Wall's *Portfolio* has been justly credited with being the first aesthetic tribute to the river scenery; it combined topographic veracity with a refined sense of beauty and was a popular and influential production.

John Hill's oldest son, John William Hill, was trained as an engraver by his father and helped him with the *Portfolio*. In 1833 he studied art in England and later settled next to his parents' property in Nyack, building what is known as The Homestead in c. 1841–45. He illustrated volumes of the state's animals for the New York State Geological Survey and worked extensively as a topographic artist, painting cities from Halifax to Havana, until he encountered John Ruskin's book *Modern Painters* in 1855. He and his son, John Henry Hill, were deeply affected by Ruskin's interest in intense detail and the necessity of painting outdoors, in front of the subject, with bright, prismatic colors. John William Hill's style changed radically: the old conventional approach was replaced by Pre-Raphaelite truth to nature. Like the French nineteenth-century landscape painter Charles François Daubigny, he built a special raft which he used to paint the light effects on the Hackensack River. Father and son became close friends of the Ruskinians Thomas C. Farrer and Charles Herbert Moore, who wrote about them.[6]

The work of both John William Hill and his son was largely done around Nyack, especially from the late 1860s, but they also made sketching trips to the Catskills and New England. John Henry Hill was also a topographic artist: in 1898 he accompanied Clarence King on his Fortieth Parallel Survey, an expedition that included the eminent documentary photographer T. H. O'Sullivan.[7] The Hills' unpretentious, rustic buildings, as well as the views of their environments, demonstrated the inherent modesty of this family of artists and their closeness to the rural community of neighboring Dutch farmers (fig. 2).

Another topographic artist literally drawn to the river was the English-born Robert Havell, Jr., best known today as the engraver of watercolor drawings by John James Audubon. After completing the illustrations for

2. A. C. Langmuir
THE HARVEY HOUSE AND GROUNDS. Sept. 4, 1924
Gelatin silver photograph, 8 x 10″
Hastings Historical Society, N.Y.

3. Anonymous
THE HAVELL HOUSE, OSSINING. 1841
Albumen silver photograph, 8½ x 7¼″
Ossining Historical Society, N.Y.

Audubon's monumental *Birds of America* in England in 1834, Havell and his family followed Audubon to America. He was fond of taking his family on sketching trips along the Hudson, and on one of these occasions they casually bid on, and obtained, a parcel of land at a country auction in Ossining. Havell designed his house, Rocky Mount, high above the river and painted and sketched many views from this site and others nearby. He also painted river scenes on the interior walls of his belvedere. In all of these he depicted a serene setting, with a sensitivity to atmosphere and the particularity of the site. These panoramic views (see cat. no. *22*) are sweeping, carefully observed, and somewhat naive. In 1857 he moved to a more high-style Victorian house in Tarrytown, now destroyed, and continued to paint panoramas of the Hudson. These were never signed, it was said, because he wished to be remembered as an engraver. Havell died in Tarrytown in 1878.[8]

Although Robert W. Weir did not build his house and studio on the Hudson, he was an important force in the documentation of the West Point area, where he lived for many years. Weir replaced Charles R. Leslie as the drawing master at West Point and moved there in 1834 to teach courses in surveying, engineering, cartography, and other military uses of drawing. The government built an extension to his house on Professors' Row for use as a studio, which had what the nineteenth-century observer Benson J. Lossing called "one of the loveliest of river and mountain views northward from the Point."[9] At least one important commercial photographer thought enough of the view and its association with the artist to issue a stereo card credited as *West Point, Up the River from Professor Weir's* (fig. 5). Soon after his move to the area, Weir became interested in landscape painting, specifically in the West Point locale, and made several panoramic views (cat. no. 4).

The military academy, located high above a bend in the river, had become a favorite spot for topographers. Although Weir was not hired to teach a sense of beauty to his charges but to give instruction in topographic and engineering drawing, some of his students, such as Seth Eastman (cat. no. 5), produced remarkably subtle

4. Anonymous
VIEW OF PROFESSOR'S ROW SHOWING R. W. WEIR'S HOUSE AND STUDIO
(SEEN AT THE FAR LEFT). n.d.
Modern copy of a 19th-century photograph, 7 1/2 x 9 1/2"
United States Military Academy Library, West Point, N.Y.

representations of the site. Weir was an ambitious and well-trained artist with a wide aesthetic range. Besides topographically accurate views of the Hudson, he painted fanciful versions, some with turreted castles, and was also interested in historical painting, genre, and even children's subject matter (for example, he illustrated *The Night before Christmas*). He designed the little chapel of the Holy Innocents just south of the Academy and recorded attractive structures on its grounds (including the picturesque ruins of Fort Putnam) and those nearby.

5. American Stereoscopic Company,
Langenheim, Loyd and Co., Phila.
WEST POINT, UP THE RIVER
FROM PROFESSOR WEIR'S. 1859
Albumen silver, photographs on stereo card,
2⅞ x 2⅞" (each image size)
United States Military Academy Library,
West Point, N.Y.

Weir's presence at West Point was also important for his fellow artists. A genial man, he was much loved by his students, family, and friends. West Point, and Weir's home especially, became a way station for artists traveling farther up the river and into the mountains. Two of his sons, John Ferguson Weir and Julian Alden Weir, became artists. John Ferguson Weir recalled visits from Cole, Durand, Henry, Gignoux, and others. His paintings of his father's studio show elaborate carved furniture, casts, papers, and canvases: the same environment Robert Weir depicted in *The Microscope*, surrounded by family and friends.[10] John Weir also lovingly painted the view from his parents' house and his father's studio (cat. no. 8). A contemporary of Weir's described its spirit:

> A studio like this . . . low in tone, rich in detail, is "like an old chapel" which the prayers of saints and the petitions of longing hearts have vitalized to an almost living quality. So here the presence of the artist, whose eye flashes, whose face lights up with kindly humor and friendliness, creates an atmosphere not to be found in the city studio or in the life of the fashionable painter. It has repose, culture, breadth of vision.[11]

Robert Weir, as an artist of some national reputation, exemplifies the position of many of these artists, whose aesthetic ambition was combined with a related interest or expertise in scientific (or even popular) visual forms. This diversity of approach is even clearer with Thomas Cole, who, as the preeminent Hudson River artist, made landscape painting a high aesthetic and moral pursuit. He was fascinated not only by painting but by architecture, music, and poetry, to all of which he contributed significantly. He was, moreover, interested in the depiction of topography, in popular panoramas, and in photography, which reverberated in his art. As a consequence, he was deeply interested not only in modifying his house, studios, and landscape around the town of Catskill, New York, but also in documenting that environment. His presence inspired a great posthumous recording of the site by his friends and younger artists, as well as Durand's eloquent painting, *Kindred Spirits*, memorializing Cole's favored mountain site in the Catskills, Kaaterskill Clove.

At his death in 1848 at the age of forty-seven, Cole was generally acknowledged as the originator of the Hudson River School. He had settled in Catskill in 1836, after several years of painting trips to that area. His first momentous visit to the Hudson River in 1825 resulted in three paintings, placed in the window of a paint store—G. W. Bruen's shop—which were admired and purchased by three older artists, John Trumbull, William Dunlap, and Asher B. Durand. With this gesture of interest and support, the so-called Hudson River School was initiated.

Cole lived in his wife's family house, which was happily situated for an artist. At that time the property included much more than the small parcel of land that surrounds the main house today. Cole converted one of the farm buildings for his studio, and later, drawing on his architectural background, designed and built an attractive larger studio with windows from floor to ceiling, completed in 1846. He would often walk up the knoll toward the river to sketch that view (fig. 6) or the view across the river (cat. no. 13), then turn his back to it and walk toward the mountains, especially favoring views of North Mountain, where Catskill Mountain House stood. At other times he would walk toward the Catskill Creek. Cole's property was close to the Long Dock landing, where the creek emptied into the Hudson, an especially beautiful area and still-favored picnic ground that shortly after his death became known as Cole's Grove.

Cole's attitude to the actuality of nature was fascinatingly ambivalent. Although his friend and biographer, Louis Legrand Noble, ascribed his greatness to "truthfulness to nature," Cole preferred to wait for "time to draw a veil over the common details."[12] He is usually credited with inspiring a national tradition in landscape painting, which was neatly aligned with cultural (and, later, even political) concerns in America. For Cole, to be truthful

6. Thomas Cole
LONG DOCK, CATSKILL LANDING ON THE HUDSON RIVER. 1847
Pen and ink on paper, 10¼ x 15⅞"
Albany Institute of History and Art, N.Y.

in art meant to ascribe moral rather than physical truth to an ideal. The veil over details suggests an inner, imaginative reality. As Barbara Novak has so perceptively suggested, there were two poles to Cole's art: one respecting a topographic sense of place, the other more inward turning, that of a religious European Romantic. He was, after all, eighteen when he came to the United States, and his conventions of landscape were essentially based on English pictorial ideas of the picturesque and the beautiful, grounded in a profound admiration for Claude Lorraine and Salvator Rosa. Cole designed Italianate details for his house and studio and a Gothic edifice for St. Luke's Episcopal Church in Catskill—clearly because these styles had strong associations for him. He also painted religious allegories while continuing his interest in topographic representation.

The year of Cole's death, Frederic Church, the only pupil Cole ever took, sketched the residence of his former mentor with exactitude and also painted an extravagant fancy of Cole's grave, *To the Memory of Thomas Cole*. In 1844 Church had come from his native Hartford to study with Cole for two years. As he wrote to his future teacher:

> I have frequently heard of the beautiful and romantic scenery about Catskill; once I passed near there, but so long ago that I remember nothing but the abrupt bluffs and lofty heights which characterize one of its grandest features, and it would give me the greatest pleasure to accompany you in your rambles about the place, observing nature in all her various appearances.[13]

For most of his active years, though based in New York City, Church retained a strong interest in the mid-Hudson Valley, visiting the Catskill Mountain House and painting such sites as Catskill Creek and the Kaaterskill Clove until he discovered the exotic scenery that made him famous. After his marriage in 1860, Church bought and began to develop his Hudson property, remaining at Olana all his life.

7. *Attrib.* Frederic E. Church
THE ALEXANDER THOMPSON HOUSE, OUTBUILDINGS AND THOMAS COLE STUDIO.
1848. Pencil on paper, 6¾ x 10¼″
New York State Office of Parks, Recreation
and Historic Preservation, Olana State Historic Site, Hudson, N.Y.

Still extant are several paintings and drawings of Cole's property, made by his friends and by some who admired but never actually knew him. There is a sense of holy memorial in the Cropsey drawings of Cole's house and studios, executed five years after the artist's death. Cropsey's training in architecture, which he intermittently practiced at various times in his career, must have made him particularly appreciative of Cole. Lauding Cole as the preeminent painter of his time in an 1845 essay, "Natural Art,"[14] Cropsey also stressed the greater value of rendering the actuality of nature, of being "faithful" to it, rather than approaching it with imagination. On a visit to Cole's property in 1850, he wrote to his wife:

> We entered; it seemed as if Mr. Cole would be in in a few minutes for every thing remains as when he last left painting. The picture he last painted on yet stands on the Easel. The brushes he painted with that last day are there; his paint table looks as when he was there. . . . Though the man has departed, yet he has left a spell behind him that is not broken, as you may sit there upon the sofa, and look upon his works, we will feel more than ever the devotion, genius and spirit of the man. Every thing breaths [sic] so much candor of will, truth of purpose, and love of the refined and beautiful, that we feel a kind of reverence there, we instinctively feel like taking off our hats, when we enter although He is not there.[15]

Cropsey's appreciation of Cole's spirit pays homage to the older artist's deep religious mission, shared by his younger contemporaries. Cole was an artistic saint, and thus his environment became a shrine. Cropsey shared with Durand not only a reverence for Cole but also a clearly observed view of nature, often drawn (as Cole rarely did) in plein air. Cropsey's friend the collector and artist John M. Falconer accompanied him on a visit to Cole's home. Interested in the documentation of old houses, Falconer made paintings of the house and studio, possibly as a result of this visit.[16]

Another artist-documentor, Benjamin B. G. Stone, made his permanent home in the city of Catskill in 1854 and rented Cole's studio for a time.[17] After studies with the artist Benjamin Champney, he worked with Cropsey and by 1853 had made his first visit to the Cole house. There he became persuaded of Cole's meaning for him and Catskill's attraction to him. A very modest man, he earned much of his income from reproductions of his careful drawings of picturesque sights in the Catskills and by selling work to guests at the Catskill Mountain House or the Hotel Kaaterskill, another grand hotel in the area. Many of the Prang reproductions of Stone's drawings on small visiting-card-size stock are still plentiful in the area. Sanford Gifford, one of his artist acquaintances, praised Stone for his "very beautiful and excellent representation [of the Kaaterskill Falls]. I have seen a great many pictures of this beautiful spot but I have never seen a more truthful one."[18] His drawings are a graceful feature of Lionel De Lisser's tour guide of the region, *Picturesque Catskills* (1894), perfectly complementing De Lisser's sensitive photographs of Cole's environment and other picturesque sites of the region.[19]

The view from Cole's hill toward the river was painted in 1863 by Thomas Farrer, an English emigré who had studied with John Ruskin and was eager to convert Americans to his new manner of conceiving art. Among those Farrer influenced was Charles Herbert Moore, who had moved to Catskill by 1861, where he designed and built his house.[20] By then he had produced a fresh and distinctive painting, *The Catskills in Spring* (cat. no. 42), from a vantage point close to his property. His property was slightly north of Thomas Cole's, with a spectacular view of the river and mountains. By 1866 Moore was paying rent to Theodore Cole for the use of his father's studio and was painting careful views of Cole's house and studio (see cat. no. 46).

These relationships are all the more interesting because the American Pre-Raphaelite organization, the Association for the Advancement of Truth in Art, led by Farrer, was united under the principle of truth to nature. Many of their pictures were carefully painted outdoors. Their work was criticized for its lack of art, its gross and uncivilized naturalism, and its common resemblance to photography. Defying official taste, these artists openly and harshly criticized the Hudson River School, specifically condemning Thomas Cole's painting as "hopeless imbecility,"[21] dependent as it was on European conventions of the picturesque and the beautiful. One of the paintings they criticized severely was Cole's *Catskill Creek* (now in the New-York Historical Society), a very accurate rendition of the site.[22]

8. Benjamin B. G. Stone. A PEEP AT THE HUDSON AT THE HOME OF THOMAS COLE.
1896. Oil on canvas grisaille, 7⅜ x 10½″
Allen Memorial Art Museum, Oberlin College, Ohio. Gift of Charles F. Olney, 04.1205

9. Anonymous
EMILY COLE INSIDE HER FATHER'S SECOND STUDIO.
c. 1900. Albumen silver photograph, 4¾ x 7⅞″
Albany Institute of History and Art, N.Y.

Moore's *The Catskills in Spring* was done from a vantage point not far from the view Cole had chosen for many of his pictures. However, Moore's painting is a kind of gloss not only on the older man's work specifically but on the early Hudson River School in general—a revision, perhaps, of their view of Cole in the light of truth. The sky's lightness and airiness are certainly new, as is the particularity of the scene.

Farrer's work, clear and fresh, is among the most lyric of the American Pre-Raphaelite group. He must have visited Moore, and later these two seem to have enjoyed painting expeditions to such nearby places as Faun's Leap and the creek—spots also favored by their Pre-Raphaelite colleague John William Hill. By 1866 Moore's work had become increasingly careful and truthful, for example, *Valley of the Catskills*, a snow scene from a slightly more northern vantage point and closer to his home. *The Valley of the Catskill from Jefferson Hill* is a further articulation of this scene.[23]

Moore was particularly fond of the rustic bridge in Leeds (the original Catskill) located upstream on the creek. He praised its unpretentious, utilitarian grace in a letter to his patron, Charles Eliot Norton, in 1866 and again in an article he wrote for the *Atlantic Monthly* in 1889.[24] This bridge, as well as other local sights, was photographed by Robert Fulton Ludlow, a descendant of his namesake, whose artistic talent he shared. Although Ludlow was a painter, his more memorable artistic expression was photography. He undoubtedly used his glass-plate camera as a memory aid for his many paintings of old houses in Columbia County and environs—perhaps the most important is a view of Irving's Sunnyside. Sensitive to the history of his environment, he documented such special places as Mount Merino and Cole's studio barn, as well as his own home, one of the most beautiful Federal period houses in Claverack. (He also collected photographs.)[25]

Of the mid-century artists who established themselves in the Hudson region, many chose to build homes in the Italianate style. Far from a merely fashionable choice, it was done because Italy had played a decisive role in the lives of many of them. Cole's studio was the first example, followed by Thomas Rossiter's house in Cold Spring, Morse's in Poughkeepsie, and certain features of the homes of Palmer and Havell, and Gifford's belvedere studio.

Although these artists chose to live in environments rich in associations with the Old World, with intangible fantasy, they were also concerned with documenting the here and now. Photography occupied a special place in the careers of Morse and Rossiter and was an important tool for Gifford and Palmer. In some ways, photographs replaced the topographic inclinations of the earlier artists and provided a deeper documentary memory.

After meeting Louis Daguerre in Paris, Morse wrote a letter to the editor of the *New York Observer*, printed on April 20, 1839—four months after Daguerre's invention was announced to the French Academy of Sciences. Morse called the daguerreotypes he saw "one of the most beautiful discoveries of the age."[26] His response to the daguerreotype was first and foremost that of an artist, and his position as both an artist of considerable stature and a scientist was to influence American acceptance of this medium, not only as a scientific achievement but as a tool of potential beauty.[27]

Anticipating photography's use as an aid to artists, Morse declared to the National Academy of Design in 1840:

> By a simple and easily portable apparatus, he [the artist] can now furnish his studio with *fac-similie* sketches of nature, landscapes, buildings, groups of figures, &c., scenes selected in accordance with his own peculiarities of taste; but not, as heretofore, subjected to his imperfect, sketchy translations into crayon or Indian ink drawings, and occupying days, and even weeks, in their execution; but painted by Nature's self with a minuteness of detail, which the pencil of light in her hands alone can trace, and with a rapidity, too, which will enable him to enrich his collection with a superabundance of materials and not copies. . . .[28]

How different, how factual are Morse's responses as compared with the essentially ecstatic, even religious response to nature of Cole, Cropsey, and Weir. Curiously, Morse shared not only a taste for actuality with the Hudson River painters but also a high ideality, in his case manifested in the mythological subjects in his early work and his later preference for Italianate architecture. The presence of such a forceful figure in the mid-Hudson Valley (even though essentially a summer resident) and his persuasive defense of photography may very well have encouraged the younger Valley artists to collect and even make photographs. Rossiter's personal collection of art and artifacts included hundreds, perhaps even thousands, of photographs of just the sort that Morse describes.[29] Cole's modest holdings complemented his collection of engravings. Mid-century painters amassed photographs of works of art as well as views of European sites and of their immediate environment.

For those artists attracted to the Hudson for its civilized beauty, the impulse to document their site through photographs or paintings must have been most natural. The melding of ideal and real is made tangible in contemporary photographs of Morse's Locust Grove. Rossiter documented Cold Spring and his immediate environment by painting his house and grounds, in some cases including a small figure contemplating the pastoral scene—a conceit from European art. A sense of ideal as well as past time (associated with photography) lingers in some of these paintings, particularly the family group on the piazza (cat. no. 44). Rossiter, who spent time in Italy as a young artist, chose Italianate architecture for his home, but the surrounding landscape was made deliberately picturesque.

> The house was nearly completed, but the grounds around were in a state of transition from the ruggedness of the wilderness to the mingled aspects of Art and Nature, formed by the direction of good taste. It is a delightful place for the artist to reside, commanding one of the most extensive and picturesque views to be found in all that Highland region. The river is seen broken into lakes, in appearance; and on all sides rise in majesty the everlasting hills. Only at one point—a magnificent vista between Mt. Taurus and the Storm King—can the world without be seen.[30]

Rossiter lived at Cold Spring during his last years, from 1860 to his death in 1871, but a much greater commitment to the region was exhibited by the younger artist, Sanford R. Gifford, who was born in Hudson, New York. Like many artists of his generation, Gifford had a studio in the Tenth Street Studio Building in New York City, but unlike them maintained close ties to the upstate area. In 1870 he built a belvedere on top of the family home on Sixth and Diamond streets in Hudson, which he used as a studio. The great number of local subjects found in the artist's estate (and exhibited in his memorial show at the Metropolitan Museum of Art in 1881) suggests that he used this studio and another in the mountains regularly.

A link stronger than the familial kept Gifford returning to Hudson. As a young man he was fond of solitary hikes in the area and especially liked climbing Mount Merino to gaze at the river and the Catskill Mountains beyond. At the artist's memorial service his friend Worthington Whittredge described how one day, in an effort to determine his future, Gifford noticed Cole's house across the way, "around which we may well believe there was a halo of light that morning."[31] Though this story has an air of fantasy, Cole's presence in Catskill was of major importance to young Gifford. He was drawn to the wilderness of the Catskills, where he had a small cottage, and to the region around Hudson, including its marshes and Claverack Creek. He was also sensitive to the midsummer haze of the Hudson Valley. Indeed, views from his belvedere studio may very well have intensified the atmospheric luminescence he was so gifted in depicting.

Gifford's precision and limpid tonality during the years he was affected by Luminism, in the 1860s to the end of his life in 1880, may have been suggested by photography, a medium he collected. He had worked alongside the photographer W. H. Jackson on Hayden's 1870 western expedition and must have been familiar with Civil War photographs and the Stoddard images around the Lake George area. Gifford and other painters may have been attracted by photography's limitations during that period. In the wet-plate process the photographic emulsion was too slow to stop the motion of moving water, for example, and often the sky was overexposed, leaving it a blank abstract shape. The limpid light effects seen in photographs of the period—especially in water—and the design of the sky may in some cases have enhanced Gifford's Luminist instincts.[32]

Photography played a major role in the lives of the sculptor Erastus Dow Palmer, his son Walter Launt Palmer, and their close friend across the river, Frederic Church. By 1865 the Palmer family spent summers in their Van Wie's Point home south of Albany, named Appledale. There Palmer had constructed a family retreat and studio, where he also arranged the planting of trees. His matter-of-fact idealism, based on a keen visual memory of what he saw, naturally inclined him to an interest in photography, and the many photographs of his family, the environs, the house and grounds depict a combination of the practical and the ideal. Many of these images were by professional photographers. One of them, F. J. Haines of Albany, made a series of seventeen stereo views that were obviously intended for sale. Haines must have considered Palmer a local celebrity, but he has depicted a wealthy, conventional family enjoying their summer pleasures[33] (cat. no. 49).

Both Palmers, father and son, collected and commissioned photographs, and young Walter often took photographs himself, which were used as studies for his paintings. The elder Palmer sent photographs of his sculptures to his friends and probably used the medium initially as a way of documenting and informing the public of his work—since he lived in Albany, relatively far from the art center of New York.

Walter grew up among his father's friends, knowing such painters as McEntee, Kensett, Charles Loring Elliott, and Church. He studied with Church beginning in 1870 and continued irregularly for perhaps two years, later sharing a studio in New York with his former teacher and traveling with him to Mexico in 1895. Young Palmer paid homage to Church's environment in an intimate painting of a bend in the road to Olana in snow. Palmer made his reputation painting winter scenes: casual and intimate views of icy brooks and banks heavy with snow. His loosely brushed paintings of nature were inspired by his contact with Barbizon painting, but his early work is much more highly detailed. As a young artist, he painted many interiors, both of Albany sites and of Appledale, with the precision of a person familiar with photography (cat. no. 50). Indeed, Walter Palmer's own collection included many photographs, some purchased, others taken by himself as studies for his work. These include interiors and exterior views of houses, Barbizon-type scenery in France (many by Achille Quinet), and scores of snow scenes. Some of these are cyanotypes, whose blue color may have inspired him to paint the blue shadows for which he became famous.[34]

On July 15, 1881, Church wrote to his old friend Erastus Dow Palmer:

> I expect in August a Photographer to come here and take a series of views, some including the House so I wish to have a few details finished—such as the enclosed verandah by the nursery—etc. This photographer—who is very skillful—agrees to work for me supplying everything for $7—per day and 50 cents extra for each view taken—He expects to take from 6 to 8 views per day. I thought it would be pleasant to have an album of some of the more interesting views and also pictures of the House inside and out—I think when the photographer comes I shall need you to help "lay out" the views.[35]

Church, of all the painters in the area, was the one most visibly interested in the architecture, landscape design, and documentation of his environment at Olana, near Hudson. He was the most gifted artist of the area to take an interest in extending the parameters of art. Photography inspired his "stereographic vision," according to one historian. He was familiar with, and collected, all kinds of photographs: portraits of his friends, expeditionary views, images of Europe, North Africa, and the Holy Land, as well as daguerreotypes of Niagara, stereo views, tiny *cartes de visite*, and large-format photographs. He was also interested in the panorama and marked a passage in his copy of Alexander von Humboldt's famous *Cosmos* that explicitly mentions Robert Barker's panoramas and Daguerre's "discoveries" as aiding the understanding of the particular characteristics of "the great enchantment of Nature."[36] Perhaps Church epitomized the combination of factual observation and the ideal, and it is not surprising that his use of the photograph is the most thorough and long-lasting of the Hudson River artists. Photography reinforced the idealization of nature through the scientifically exact rendering he sought.

Church's vast collection of photographs included Désiré Charnay's Mayan ruins, Giacomo Brogi's views of Florence, William James Stillman's book of the Acropolis, and images closer to home by W. H. Jackson, John Moran, Eadweard Muybridge, and many others. Clearly his primary interest was in exotic subjects, as one might expect of a man who designed a house of supreme (and distinctly oriental) fantasy on the banks of the Hudson. There is a vast array of views of Olana itself: interior as well as exterior, professional and amateur. Though many were probably made by Church's son, Louis, they reflect Church's intense care for his house, studio, and grounds. The extensive restoration at Olana has been made possible because of the quantity of photographic documentation of the site done in Church's lifetime or shortly thereafter.

The local environment of the Rondout section of Kingston, as well as the interior of the Catskills, was very important to Jervis McEntee. He was born in Kingston, studied with Church, and was a good friend of Gifford, with whom he traveled to Europe. Although there is no specific evidence for McEntee's interest in photography, a deep attachment to his environment has been documented. He painted many views of Rondout, specifically a charming, modest view of the scene from the window of his studio, which had been designed by his brother-in-law, Calvert Vaux. McEntee's view matches Vaux's illustration of the structure in his *Villas and Cottages* (cat. no. 27).

Church's great rival, Albert Bierstadt, built a house on the Hudson at Irvington in 1865 and named it Malkasten to commemorate his German artistic heritage. Soon after, he recorded the view from his home. Bierstadt, however, lived in Malkasten only periodically. Because it was large and cold during the winter, he rented it regularly from 1869 until it was finally destroyed by fire in 1882. The mansion was included in a series on Hudson River houses (including Church's Olana) published by Martha Lamb in the *Art Journal* in 1875. It was photographed quite extensively by Edward Bierstadt, one of the painter's two photographer brothers.[37] Albert Bierstadt was intimately concerned with photography and such visual forms as lantern slides and panoramas, particularly in his youth, and had worked closely with his two brothers. Such a close relationship with the medium clearly affected his dramatic, sharply observant style. Thus the Bierstadt mansion was documented as the spectacular home it was, and for the grand (as well as more intimate) views it afforded, but these images lack the intimacy or sense of personal rootedness found in views of the Palmer residence, Appledale. Perhaps appropriately the very best shows a vast and wild panorama of the river seen from Bierstadt's property, high above it.

By the end of the century, artists' communities were established along the Hudson and in the Catskills. The first of these, Cragsmoor, near Ellenville, was settled by Edward Lamson Henry, an artist remembered today more for his antiquarianism than his purely aesthetic accomplishments. He arrived there for the first of his almost annual summer visits in 1879 and five years later bought property and began to construct a house of his own design, formed with decorative objects salvaged from demolished buildings in New York City.

Henry was not only attracted to the spectacular views from the mountaintop location but also admired the old fieldstone farm buildings and primitive log-cabin structures, which reminded him of an earlier, simpler existence. As part of his mania for amassing objects from the past—Henry's collection of eighteenth-century American costumes is now at the Brooklyn Museum—and as an aid to his paintings of eighteenth-century life, he turned to photography. A resident of the area, Le Grand Botsford, was hired to photograph Henry's paintings and also sold the artist photographs of views. Henry acquired an extensive collection of photographs, including notable examples by John Moran, son of the painter Thomas Moran, and many documenting colonial architecture in Boston, New York, and Philadelphia.

Henry was also a photographer. Undoubtedly he used a camera as an aid to his paintings. In several cases he painted almost exact copies of a photograph, and sometimes he painted over a photograph or even over a photograph of a painting.[38] The most interesting images by far are documents of his house and garden, apple trees in bloom, and friends. In most cases they are lyrical, boldly seen and composed, and more individual than the paintings made directly after them (see cat. no. 71).

Henry's enthusiasm for Cragsmoor persuaded Frederick W. Dellenbaugh to visit in 1881 and eventually settle there. Dellenbaugh was an explorer and artist of moderate talents who had accompanied Major J. Wesley Powell on his second expedition down the Colorado River in 1871–73. He wrote vividly about this experience in *A Canyon Voyage* (1908), illustrated with many photographs by E. O. Beaman and John Hillers.[39] He was also a photographer himself.[40] Dellenbaugh's paintings are mainly documentary in nature, records of his trips to faraway places complementing his writings. Like so many other artists, Dellenbaugh expanded his aesthetic field of vision. He became known as the chief architect of the Cragsmoor community, using details from demolished buildings assembled, collage-like, in a Queen Anne–style context. Dellenbaugh and another Cragsmoor artist, Charles C. Curran, were also deeply interested in their large gardens.

There is no evidence that George Inness, Jr. (son of the more famous artist) was particularly fascinated by photography, though perhaps because of the grand scale of his mansion, Chetolah, there are more photographs of this structure than of any other on the Cragsmoor mountaintop[41] (cat. no. 78). When he built Chetolah, about 1901, Inness shared the design responsibilities with a professional architect and attended to the design of the grounds.

The Onteora Park community, whose guiding spirit was Candace Wheeler, was another location where artists often became their own (and one another's) architects and designers. Candace Wheeler and her daughter, Dora Wheeler Keith, were professional textile designers and artists. An extravagant lover of flowers (the Candace Wheeler Wildflower Garden was created at the library in her memory), Candace Wheeler decorated her own house with images of flowers, and her daughter painted the surrounding landscapes in the studio nearby. Onteora Park was a summer residential club organized by Wheeler, initially with only members of her family. However, soon friends, among them painters, writers, and actors, either settled or came to the mountaintop for extensive visits. Documents that survive are essentially records of people—for example, Mark Twain's visit to the colony, or the artist J. Carroll Beckwith's portrait of Annie Vail in his studio.[42] Beckwith and his wife were avid photographers, and though they did photograph their summer house and the studio, their most interesting images were of people, particularly Beckwith's studies of his wife. The chief exception to this documentation of the active social life of the Onteora colony was a series of views made from around the area known as the Artists' Rock and the nearby Artist's Seat. Candace Wheeler was careful to find and dedicate her Artists' Rock in memory of the Hudson River painters who had been her friends and had awakened her to the attractive scenery in the Catskills. Besides the paintings of G. L. Reid and Beckwith, some of the photographs of this location are especially sensitive[43] (see fig. 10).

10. Anonymous
VIEW OF ARTIST'S SEAT (NEAR ARTISTS' ROCK). n.d.
Gelatin silver photograph on postcard, 3¼ x 5¼″
Courtesy of Onteora Club, N.Y.

Another artist whose home in the Catskills was documented at this time was the sculptor John Quincy Adams Ward. He had a fishing lodge at Peekamoose Mountain, next door to his associate, J. W. Wentworth, and his wife, the artist Celia Wentworth. In 1893, Lionel De Lisser, the photographer and author, visited this thinly populated corner of the Catskills and found Ward's stone house with its plain facade, which the sculptor was just beginning to enlarge and decorate. This region of Greene County was particularly spectacular, featuring a gorge, high mountain, and a dammed-up river forming a deep, cold pool (fig. 11). After decorating the old stone structure with fanciful gables and fancy cut bargeboards, Ward had the result photographed by C. B. Tubbs; it was a large, handsome, and atmospheric picture (fig. 12). A sometime friend and partner of the Peekamoose Club, A. W. Dimock, presented Ward with an album of views of the property and activities of the club members, which are appropriately lighthearted.

The gray, smoky, tonal quality in Tubbs's photograph of Peekamoose and its sense of romantic, approachable wildness are typical of the more sensitive and private, less objective photography of the end of the century. This approach was called Pictorialism because it sought to redirect photography as an art of picture-making rather than the mere static and mechanical copying of a subject. These photographers stressed close-toned atmosphere and careful (often Japanese-inspired) compositions, and they frequently chose as subjects nudes or

11. R. Lionel De Lisser
WARD PROPERTY, PEEKAMOOSE MOUNTAIN
Page size 13½ x 10¾". From the book *Picturesque Ulster*, 1893
Courtesy of Professor and Mrs. William B. Rhoads

women in diaphanous garments. This photography is ultimately a reflection of the more intimate and personal painting of the period, often referred to as Tonalism, in which artists turned away from the objective and descriptive style of the Hudson River School.

12. C. B. Tubbs
JOHN QUINCY ADAMS WARD'S HOUSE AT PEEKAMOOSE. c. 1885
Silver gelatin photograph, 10^{13}/$_{16}$ x 13^{13}/$_{16}$"
Albany Institute of History and Art, N.Y.

Though not actually a Tonalist himself, George Inness was a seminal figure in this change of outlook. While Cole was reared in the conventions of the picturesque, and the following generation aspired to a greater scientific accuracy—without diminishing the high moral content—Inness was influenced by Barbizon painting, by its loose brushwork, tonalities, and casual, intimate subject matter, especially the closely seen pastorals and farmlike views. Whereas Church, Cropsey, Moore, and perhaps even Gifford retained a religious ideality, Inness was more personally expressive, less puritanical, but still deeply interested in the religiosity of art.

Inness had a long relationship with the Hudson Valley, though he painted specific Hudson landscapes relatively rarely. As his biographer Nicolai Cikovsky, Jr., has stated, Inness's art was inspired more by art than by the experience of nature, more attuned to Italy and France than to America. Not fond of nature's wildness like the Hudson River School artists, he preferred what he called "civilized landscape."[43] Thus it is curious to find him painting for several periods of time at Leeds, near Catskill, the home of Cole, at the foot of the mountains that attracted the Hudson River artists. Could he, like Farrer and Moore, have wanted to remake that very landscape so rich in artistic associations? He showed a more concentrated interest in the Hudson landscape after several summers at Milton, about 1879 through the early 1880s. This coincided with a period when he dedicated his efforts to the figure. The paintings made near the house and grounds of his hostess and patron, Asia Hallock, and the picturesque old barn Inness used as a studio often depict children or farm people. But his preference for landscape also asserted itself. The view from Milton toward the river is a close, personal one, not grand and distant (see cat. no. 60).

Inness's artistic style became part of the general move to paintings of expressive mood, away from the spectacular views of the Hudson River School. The little artist's colony of Pakatakan at Arkville, including Alexander H. Wyant, J. Francis Murphy, E. Loyal Field, and Parker Mann—shared this commitment to a personal, even moody expression in landscape. Like earlier painters, they documented their carefully created personal environments, which are a full expression of their aesthetic ideals.

Murphy was the first to settle at Arkville. He and his wife, the painter Adah Clifford Murphy, were very much involved in the building of their first structure in 1887, the meadow-like Weedwild landscape, and the buildings that followed. Even though Murphy's work is largely nonspecific, there are several paintings that clearly depict a precise Arkville location and many that describe the undulant hills, gentle plains, and modest farmlike buildings characteristic of the area. Both Murphys were careful documentors of the buildings, gardens, and views. Many friends enhanced their life at Arkville. Artists came to build there—the Wyants, the Manns, the Fields, whose houses still stand, and others came to stay at the Pakatakan Inn or had homes that are now destroyed, such as Ernest Rost, Frank Russell Green, and Charles Smillie. In the summer of 1887, when the "Shanty" studio was constructed, Mrs. Murphy described how Rost and Smillie both took photographs of her and the building. She became interested in the process, started developing prints that year, and at some point became deeply involved with photography. Some of her photographs were studies for her paintings. Adah Murphy's studio at Arkville was outfitted with a darkroom, and a considerable number of her glass-plate negatives remain. Her tonal images celebrate the simplicity of the setting and the harmony of nature in the summer (see Chap. 4, fig. 14).

Although none of the many photographs in the Murphy archives is directly attributable to Francis Murphy himself, the Corot-like compositions of pastoral settings certainly reflect his painting interests. The Murphy buildings became a local tourist attraction and were the subject of a series of postcard views published by 1905.[44]

Although Wyant arrived at Arkville late in life (he built his house there in 1889 and died in 1892), he made scores of paintings of local subjects—landscapes, buildings, and close examinations of the geography and characteristic terrain (see Chap. 4, fig. 20). Rost is described as making a "soft, shadowy photograph, almost like a painting" of young Alec Wyant for Mrs. Wyant, and there are many other photographs of the Wyant presence at Arkville, as well as works by other artists of the colony. Perhaps the best are Parker Mann's view of the Wyant house (cat. no. 93) and an etching and monotype by Field, also of the Wyant house (fig. 13). Though Murphy was the first to arrive, Wyant was recognized as the more important figure, and rather like Cole's pres-

13. E. Loyal Field
THE WYANT HOUSE. n.d.
Etching, 6 x 8″
Courtesy of a private collection

14. *Attrib.* Adah Clifford Murphy
LOUISE HUNTINGTON COLLINS
IN MURPHY GARDEN,
ARKVILLE, N.Y. c. 1890
Gelatin silver photograph, 4¾ x 3¾″
Emerson Crosby Kelly Papers, Archives of American Art,
Smithsonian Institution, Washington, D.C.

ence at Catskill, Wyant's environment was recorded by friends and admirers. Both Field and Mann documented their own structures, those of the community, and the Pakatakan landscapes.

For artists, more than for most people, the choice of a place to live and work—and of the buildings they constructed or modified to meet their needs—was particularly meaningful as an extension of their aesthetic interests. This impulse was accompanied by a desire to document what they saw and made. Photography emerged as a powerful tool in American life by the time Cole settled in Catskill. The medium continued to interest the Hudson River artists, sometimes not only for its record-making value but also because it could be used as an aid in their painting. By the close of the century, photography had become widespread and could be modified to suit different aesthetic needs. Thus Gifford, familiar with the expeditionary work in the Far West, along with Bierstadt and Church, used the medium for its powerful objectivity, while Henry, the collector, used it for historical verification. Later artists, such as Wyant and Murphy, found it a vehicle for mood. Not surprisingly, like the arrangement and design of their own environments, the way they recorded these charmed places was defined by their aesthetic inclinations.

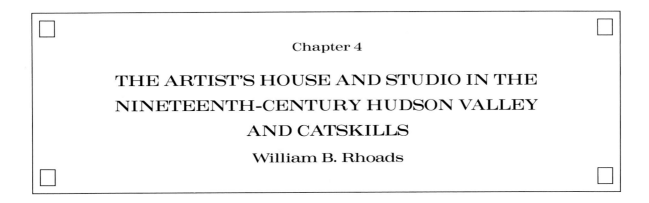

Chapter 4

THE ARTIST'S HOUSE AND STUDIO IN THE NINETEENTH-CENTURY HUDSON VALLEY AND CATSKILLS

William B. Rhoads

I n 1885 a writer describing "The Summer Haunts of American Artists" found most striking the "picket-line of studios" bordering each side of the Hudson River, ranging from the "imposing" residences of Frederic E. Church and Albert Bierstadt to the more modest quarters of Thomas Cole and the "mere gypsy booths, or bivouacs in barns and venerable canal-boats which have outlived their days of commercial usefulness and now luxuriantly devote their declining years to Art." Finally there were "in the Catskills . . . artistic campers and trampers whose entire summer's outfit might be fastened in a pair of shawl-straps."[1]

Church's Olana is justly renowned as the finest surviving artist's studio-house from nineteenth-century America, yet there were many others in the Hudson Valley and Catskills that are less well known but deserve study. Some, like Olana, were designed primarily by their artist-owners and represent architectural statements comparable to the artists' works in oil and canvas. Most, like Olana, were built for landscape painters on lofty sites that offered panoramic views. The architectural styles ranged from picturesque European modes to exotic Persian (at Olana) to the early American vernacular. While the variety of styles accorded with the shifting taste of nineteenth-century America,[2] the styles often reflected the enthusiasm artists felt for particular cultures and periods.[3] Because of the public visibility of most of the studio-houses (often enhanced by contemporary publication), they also served as advertisements of the artists' taste and prosperity.[4]

Many landscapists who sketched and painted the Catskills and Hudson Valley never established residences there. Some went to boardinghouses in small Catskill villages. Palenville, at the foot of Kaaterskill Clove, has been described as "America's first art colony," because in the fall of 1848 Asher B. Durand, John F. Kensett, John W. Casilear, and Joseph Vollerming were boarding in the village.[5] Others chose the nearby Catskill Mountain House (fig. 1), whose guest register in the 1850s and 1860s included such names as Sanford Gifford, Jervis McEntee, Jasper Cropsey, Frederic E. Church, and Worthington Whittredge.[6] McEntee wrote appreciatively of the "vast view," "charming walks," "pretty drives," and "proud piazzas" of the hotel, but claimed that its high charges kept him away.[7] Still others camped in the wilds: John Jameson, Edward Gay, and Charles Moore set up a tent and rude shelter of leafy boughs in Plauterkill Clove one August about 1860 (see fig. 2).[8] The three young artists were learning to paint the landscape as Durand advised in his first "Letter on Landscape Painting"—shunning an urban studio in favor of the nearly boundless "Studio of Nature." In fact, Kaaterskill Clove had been described in 1854 as "the favorite studio of many artists."[9]

Many landscape painters tired of the search each summer for a place to stay. Palenville, while close to scenic wonders, was itself "a hamlet of the most shabby sort," as were its "two primitive way-side taverns," according to artist T. Addison Richards. Durand's son recalled that "owing to the difficulty of procuring comfortable quarters, good food, and good beds, in farmhouses and at country taverns," his father acquired a house not far from his summer sketching grounds.[10]

For painters who chose to build a country place, usually for occupation in the warmer months, the basic requirements were few and obvious enough. The site should offer good views of the landscape (a high elevation was usually sought not only for the view but also for cool breezes), while being near the steamboat or railroad to New York for contact with other artists, patrons, and dealers. The studio itself, as Horace J. Rollin pointed out

1. J. Smillie
CATSKILL MOUNTAIN HOUSE. c. 1845
Engraving (copy of original by George Harvey), 5 x 7″
Courtesy of Professor and Mrs. William B. Rhoads

2. John S. Jameson
PLAUTERKILL CLOVE. c. 1860
Oil on canvas, 9½ x 14″
Courtesy of Professor and Mrs. William B. Rhoads

in his *Studio, Field and Gallery: A Manual of Painting for the Student and Amateur*, should be large enough for the artist to observe his work from a distance; it should be tastefully adorned with attractive objects to "cultivate and refine the taste"; it should be removed from the residence for privacy and quiet; and it should have a north light unobstructed by trees.[11]

The landscape painter George Harvey was perhaps the first artist to build a picturesque house in the Hudson Valley. He had spent his first twenty years in England and returned there for study in the early 1830s, so it is not surprising that when in 1834 he built a cottage, Woodbank, on the Hastings shore "of the majestic Hudson" he designed it to be "Elizabethan," its plain marble walls accented by Gothic window frames and eaves trimmed with bargeboards. He also laid out the lawns, paths, and garden on his twenty acres in the English picturesque manner soon to be popularized by Andrew Jackson Downing.[12] The opening of a vista through the wood along the riverbank, a vista lined with classical urns and leading to a vignette of river life, was just the sort of manipulation of nature that also appealed to Downing.

Thomas Cole, the founder of the Hudson River School, first came to the Catskill Mountains to sketch in 1825 and returned in succeeding summers (except when abroad) to the village of Catskill, "where he took lodgings, and fitted up a painting room."[13] From the village it was a walk of some ten or twelve miles to his preferred sketching grounds in the vicinity of the Catskill Mountain House.

In 1836 Cole married a Catskill woman, Maria Bartow, and established his residence in the house called Cedar Grove, just north of the village, which had been built in 1815–16 by an uncle of Maria's.[14] Its Federal-style design was outmoded by the 1830s,[15] but it did possess a panoramic view of the Catskill Mountains to the west and south.

From the wide elevated piazzas that enveloped the house on three sides, Cole could gaze upon his beloved Catskills with their "varied, undulating and exceedingly beautiful outlines."[16] Later visitors such as Cropsey commented on the view from the piazzas, and within the house was "a west window, at which persons can sit and enjoy a prospect of the vally [*sic*] and the mountains which is as fine a view as can well-be found." Upstairs Cropsey was impressed by windows that extended to the floor, one "looking over trees and meadows far to the north." Nothing about the house suggested "Luxurie and wealth"; the grounds were not elegant but attractive with a flower and vegetable garden, fruit trees and vines.[17]

It was also the view and its advantages for the landscapist that struck Henry T. Tuckerman: "we can imagine no more desirable home in the country for a landscape-painter. The variety of mountain, stream, foliage, and sky ever offered to his observation, furnish[es] exhaustless materials for study; and he is doubtless indebted in no small measure for his acknowledged fidelity to nature, to these familiar opportunities."[18]

Cole was contemplating new or remodeled quarters by 1837. In 1841 he bought an acre-and-a-quarter site from his wife's uncle but delayed construction because of "hard times, and an adage which a knowing friend of mine uttered—'fools *build* houses and wise men *live* in them.' " He offered to fill his correspondent with "cakes and ale" and then lead him to "see the site of the new house, and say how magnificent *it is to be*."[19]

The artist considered himself "something of an architect"—he was so listed in *Longworth's New York City Directory*—and had made plans for the Ohio Capitol (1838) and St. Luke's Episcopal Church in Catskill (completed 1841). Consequently, he made numerous drawings of his projected residence in the towered Italian-villa style, which apparently was to be an extensive alteration and addition to Cedar Grove.[20]

In the Victorian period client and designer had a variety of historical styles from which to choose. These choices were partially regulated by the desire to relate the building to its site (the irregularity of the grounds to be reflected in the massing of the house, according to Downing),[21] and also by the associations that clung to individual styles. For A. W. N. Pugin, Richard Upjohn, and countless others the Gothic (associated with the glories of the medieval church) was the truly Christian style.

The Italian villa, on the other hand, was a secular style, associated with painters of the Italian landscape, dotted with stucco-walled, low-towered houses. The revival of the towered, asymmetrical Italian villa seems to have occurred first in England in 1802; in 1818 J. B. Papworth published a design for an Italian villa intended "as the residence of an artist." This was fitting because the villa's forms were "selected from works of pictorial beauty" by great Italian landscape painters, and so the villa conformed to what "may be termed the painter's style of building."[22]

Downing in 1841 associated the Italian style with "that land of painters and of the fine arts" and acknowledged that "he who has a passionate love of pictures and especially fine landscapes, will perhaps, very naturally, prefer the modern Italian style for a country residence." And whose passion for fine landscapes was stronger than that of the painters themselves? In his *Architecture of Country Houses* Downing illustrated the stuccoed, towered villa of "Mr. Nesfield, a landscape-painter" in suburban London.[23]

Cole, who grew up in England and returned for an extended visit in 1829, may have been influenced by English writings in his admiration of the landscape and architecture of Italy. From his Italian sojourns (1831–32, 1841–42) stem numerous landscapes enlivened with towers of the sort that also appear in the pastorals of his idol, Claude Lorraine. Cole's preference for the Italian villa was, it seems, a consequence of his enthusiasm for the paintings of Claude and the actual Italian landscape—for which he sought parallels in the Catskills. Perhaps the knowledge that it was a style suitable for the residence of a landscape painter also influenced his taste. The tower would have enhanced his view of the Catskills, but it would not have been high enough to dominate the ridge east of the house, which effectively blocked a view of the Hudson.[24]

Cole was an advocate of the Italian villa for a wide range of householders. In his "Letter to the Publick on the Subject of Architecture" (c. 1840), he found the Italian villa superior to the English-cottage style for use in America. The latter lacked the large "piazzas, deep recesses, projecting roofs . . . demanded by the American landscape and climate." The English cottage was not "broad and grand" enough to suit the American landscape, notably "the ample hills that rise from the Hudson River." The Italian villa was the practical choice: "it affords simplicity with variety and a capability of being adapted to any internal economical arrangement. . . ."[25]

Cole made do with a variety of makeshift studios before 1846. One occupied the western portion of Cedar Grove's carriage house.[26] Another he describes in an 1839 letter to his friend Durand: "Do you know that I have got a new painting-room? Mr. Thompson [his wife's uncle] has lately erected a sort of store-house, and has let me have part of it for a temporary painting-room. It answers pretty well—is somewhat larger than my old one, and being removed from the noise and bustle of the house, is really charming. . . . The walls are of unplastered brick, with the beams and timbers seen on every hand: not a bad colour this pale brick and mortar."[27]

Cole was frustrated in his attempt to live in an Italian villa in Catskill, but in 1846 he succeeded in building a new studio near Cedar Grove, described by his friend and biographer Noble as "somewhat in the Italian villa style." It did have the low-pitched hipped roof and broad eaves associated with that style but lacked a tower. Cropsey was content to label it "in the modern florid style." Again it was the view from the studio that was most remarkable. Cole, according to Noble, thought the graceful outline of the Catskill escarpment visible from the studio door resembled the base of Mount Etna, while the sunsets rivaled Italy's. However much Cole admired the American landscape, he regretted the absence of architectural monuments such as enriched Italy and Germany, and so he looked forward to the time when the Hudson would "reflect temple, and tower, and dome, in every variety of picturesqueness and magnificence."[28]

Cole never built his tower, but others did, including Samuel F. B. Morse, Thomas P. Rossiter, and Frederic Church. In 1851–52 Morse (aided by Alexander Jackson Davis) transformed Locust Grove, his symmetrical house built near Poughkeepsie in 1830, into a picturesque Italian villa.[29] In 1847, moved by the beauty of the land and its views of river and mountains, he had purchased the one hundred acres comprising Locust Grove.[30]

Morse's decision to make Locust Grove into an Italian villa was surely inspired by his love of the Italian landscape, "the land of his dreams." In 1830–31, while traversing Italy with Davis's partner, Ithiel Town, and Thomas Cole, he had drawn at least one villa.[31] Cole, in Italy in 1841, sketched with the young artist Thomas P. Rossiter, who was enthralled by Florence and Venice, especially "the sumptuous piles of architecture" on the Grand Canal. Later, between 1855 and 1857, Rossiter built an Italian Renaissance house and studio in New York designed by Richard Morris Hunt on the basis of a sketch by Rossiter. Italy also inspired Rossiter's country house south of Cold Spring, designed with quoins, deep classical cornices, and a tower-like east mass in 1860 by the artist himself. Benson J. Lossing thought it an "elegant villa" and "a delightful place for an artist to reside, commanding one of the most extensive and picturesque views to be found in all that Highland region." When Lossing visited in the 1860s, the grounds were being transformed "from ruggedness of the wilderness to the mingled aspects of Art and Nature, formed by the direction of good taste"—surely Rossiter's own. [32]

Cole believed the tower should be part of an asymmetrical composition. Others placed an Italianate cupola atop the center of a traditional five-bay house. The landscape artist Robert Havell, Jr., moved to Sing Sing (now Ossining) in 1841 and constructed such a cupola on his house, Rocky Mount. [33]

Although Sanford R. Gifford had a studio in New York City, he always considered Hudson, the town where he grew up, as "home." In 1870 he began to build a studio atop the family residence, a substantial classical-revival block. [34] Details of the studio are unclear in the only known photo, but its general form suggests that Gifford may have been inspired by belvederes atop Roman villas like those of the Villa Medici in Rome.

Gifford's friend Jervis McEntee was another artist who grew up in sight of the Catskills. As Worthington Whittredge recalled, "[McEntee's] home had always been near them and he knew every nook and corner of them and every stepping-stone across their brooks." [35] McEntee, born in Rondout (now a section of Kingston) on the Hudson in 1828, told readers of *Our Young Folks* (1866) that "since my earliest recollection I have had 'studios' in our garrets and over our carriage houses." About 1853 he built a one-room studio, designed by Calvert Vaux, on the Weinbergh, an elevation in Rondout. [36] The studio made no reference to Italy (McEntee had not yet been there) but was made ornamental and picturesque through board-and-batten construction, projecting eaves with bargeboards, and a tin roof made complex by hips, cross gable, chimney, and finials. A hooded bench built against the exterior chimney wall encouraged contemplation of the Rondout Creek and Hudson River. A flagpole attached to the house during the Civil War added still more complexity (and expressed the artist's devotion to the Union cause). [37]

On November 1, 1854, McEntee, as he recalled later, "worked all day about my new little house," and went to New York to marry Gertrude Sawyer the next day, bringing her back to Rondout, where they established their home in the studio, newly expanded with modest living quarters in the same picturesque board-and-batten style as the studio. [38] The little house was dominated by the studio (22 x 16 feet), whose most notable feature, according to Vaux, was the "height and . . . airy effect" of the interior, achieved by having the "ceiling line follow . . . the line of the roof and collar beams. All rafters are left visible, the plastering being fitted between them."

The truly noteworthy aspect of the place for Vaux was the "extended view of the Kaatskills and the Hudson." [39] McEntee also appreciated the natural spectacle around him: "From my home in the Catskills I can look down a vista of forty miles, a magnificent and commanding sight." Nevertheless, he went on, "I have never painted it; nor should I care to paint it. What I do like to paint is my impression of a simple scene in nature." [40]

McEntee's board-and-batten studio-house belonged to the Hudson Valley and to no specific European tradition, nor did the remarkable and little-known cottage built for Charles Herbert Moore. By 1862 he was acquainted with the family of Thomas Cole, whose old studio he painted in 1862. Moore was a leading American disciple of Ruskin and active in the Society for the Advancement of Truth in Art. Ruskin's great friend at Harvard, Charles Eliot Norton, offered a teaching post to the young Moore, who declined in February 1866, writing that he felt "quite permanently settled" in Catskill. "We expect to occupy a very pleasant little cottage in the spring. . . ." [41]

Although construction was delayed two or three years, the resulting cottage, the Lodge, was well sited on the ridge north of Cole's house, with views both west to the Catskills and east over the Hudson toward the Berkshires. It was an important early example of the revival of Dutch Colonial architecture, particularly expressed in the fieldstone walls, low proportions, and gambrel roof. Moore had proclaimed his enthusiasm for "old Dutch farm houses [near Catskill] which are exceedingly interesting" in his letter to Norton. [42] (Remnants of mid-nineteenth-century fashion remained in the board-and-batten gables, brackets, and window hoods.)

Moore's preference for a Dutch Colonial cottage is not surprising. His architectural associate in the Society for the Advancement of Truth in Art, Peter B. Wight, in an unsigned essay "House Building in America" (1857), insisted that "in America the only really good houses are the old farmhouses of Dutch and English type, scattered here and there over the land, testifying to the worth of simplicity, and the beauty of common-sense, in the midst of pretense and gingerbread work." Later, writing in the society's journal, *The New Path*, Wight praised the Hudson Valley Dutch farmhouses for taking "the first step in sensible construction and picturesque arrangement."[43]

Much grander than Moore's cottage, Albert Bierstadt's imposing Malkasten (1865–66) in Irvington-on-Hudson proclaimed the commercial success of its owner, best known for his large-scale western landscapes. The walls of rough bluestone gneiss rose three stories, while a fourth was enveloped by a polychrome mansard crowned with a light iron grille. Bierstadt is said to have taken five years to select the site, high on a hill above Washington Irving's diminutive Sunnyside and with a thirty-mile panorama over and beyond the Tappan Zee. [44] "It was because of his conviction that the patient and faithful study of nature is the only adequate school of landscape art that Bierstadt, like Cole and Church, fixed his abode on the banks of the Hudson," wrote Henry Tuckerman.[45] The architect, Jacob Wrey Mould, provided every level of the river-facing facades with the greatest variety of verandas, galleries, balconies, oriels, and turrets "from which the cultivated eye may rapturously survey Nature's great landscape-garden." To the north, a tremendous three-story window revealed the owner's profession.[46]

3. Anonymous
RESIDENCE OF ALBERT BIERSTADT.
6 x 4⁷⁄₈″
From *The Art Journal*, 1875, pt. 2, p. 45
New York State Library, Albany, N.Y.

The studio was spacious enough to allow study of his big canvases from a distance, especially when the twenty-foot-high doors between studio and library were thrown open to create a seventy-foot vista. Galleries some ten feet above the studio floor, reached by narrow staircases, furnished the artist with additional vantage points. The studio was meant for painting, but the "large, cheerful fireplace" encouraged conviviality, while the vast studio walls were hung with Bierstadt's own paintings as well as hunting trophies. "An artist's bedroom" was attached to the highest oriel window, while also communicating with the gallery over the studio.[47]

John Zukowsky describes Bierstadt's house as both "châteaulike" and having "plentiful Rhenish associations, such as the several turrets, granite cladding, oriel windows, and corbeled balcony." The German connection would seem understandable given the artist's German birth and training and the fact that the house, first called Hawksrest, was renamed Malkasten after a Düsseldorf artists' club. Still, Mould was English by training, and, more important, Bierstadt himself stated that his house "was of no particular style of architecture."[48]

Malkasten was one of the first American studio-houses to receive extensive publicity—clearly the splendid house not only reflected the artist's prosperity but also brought his name and taste to public notice. Bierstadt's residency, however, was short, and in 1882 the house was destroyed by fire.[49]

Bierstadt had felt obliged to turn to an architect for Malkasten's design. Downing regretted that rarely was there a "harmonious union of buildings and scenery . . . because the architect and the landscape painter are seldom combined in the same person . . . ." One such exceptional person was Jasper F. Cropsey, who had gone through a five-year architectural apprenticeship and practiced the profession intermittently.[50] In 1866, three years after returning to America from a lengthy sojourn in England, Cropsey bought forty-five acres near the village of Warwick, Orange County, and by 1869 Aladdin, his twenty-nine-room studio-house, was completed

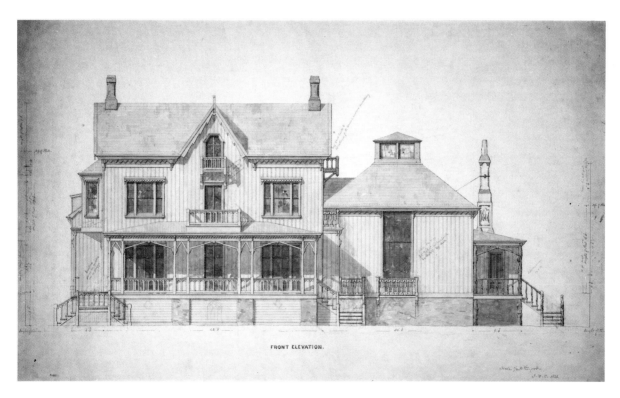

FRONT ELEVATION.

4. Jasper F. Cropsey
SUMMER COTTAGE, FRONT ELEVATION I (PROBABLY ALADDIN). 1866
Watercolor, pen, and pencil on paper, 20½ x 29⅜"
Museum of Fine Arts, Boston.
M. and M. Karolik Collection of American Paintings

to his own design. Especially when seen from the east, Aladdin was the epitome of picturesque irregularity of form. One visitor noted in 1884 that "it is a building in which every poet and painter delights, for its exterior is a picture of no little variety, in which gable and tower and balcony blend in harmonious confusion." This confusion also marked the stylistic sources, as so often occurred in architecture of the decade: an Italian tower topped by a French roof, Downingesque board-and-batten walls and Gothic arches, with a fifteenth-century Renaissance balcony.[51] Nothing was overtly Arabian to correspond with the exotic name of the property, although the sumptuously decorated interiors may have reminded Cropsey of the tale of Aladdin.

The house was sited "on the side of a hill which the Indians call Noonantum . . . mean[ing] either a 'beautiful view' or 'the hill of joy' . . . the view from the height is one of rare beauty . . . extend[ing] from the hill which rises behind Newburgh-on-the-Hudson to Port Jervis, on the Delaware, thus traversing the entire width of Orange County. . . . The country . . . stretches for miles away, varied in surface, with green meadows and pleasant cornfields on the lowlands. . . . In the far north tower the peaks of the lordly Catskills." Not far were two of Cropsey's favorite landscape subjects, Greenwood Lake and the Wawayandah Creek.[52]

"Light airy verandas and balconies" were arranged to take advantage of the view. "Curious dormer windows and picturesque balconies" opening from the bedrooms were not only oriented to the landscape beyond but were themselves "filled with flowers." The grounds near the house were terraced with beds of flowers and shrubs, while the conservatory within the house was given over to ferns and flowers.[53]

Aladdin was a gentleman's farm complete with "picturesque lodge" at the entrance, but it was the splendor of the main house's interior that made it "one of the show houses of Orange County." As such it attracted the curious public ("no one is ever refused admission") and journalists whose descriptions added luster to Cropsey's reputation as a man of taste.[54] Rooms were richly colored: stained-glass windows lit the entrance vestibule; amber and gold crystal globes adorned many of the lamps, while the dining-room ceiling had "a border painted like the illuminated margin of an ancient manuscript," and the oak dining-room furniture was designed by Cropsey "with delicate decoration in gold and red, the chairs being cushioned with purple Russia leather." The drawing room was a veritable "fairyland . . . a glow of all that is light, bright, delicate and beautiful—love-color and love-light everywhere."[55]

The studio, like Bierstadt's, belonged to the "*show* studio" category, its working function almost forgotten by visitors struck by the elaborateness of its design. For the *Home Journal* correspondent, the "grand mediaeval fire-place" was the focal point of the studio. Bric-a-brac caught the eye: three-foot bronzes of a Cavalier and a Roundhead (actually lamp bases) on the mantel shelf helped make the fireplace seem "ancient and grand"; andirons apparently from the Middle Ages were actually designed by Cropsey; the brass fender was Chinese. (Eclecticism ruled inside as well as out.) The space of the studio was impressive—thirty feet square at the base, it rose to a hipped, modestly colored, medieval timber-framed ceiling and lantern some thirty feet high. There was a large north window with adjustable walnut blinds, a western alcove for Cropsey's writing desk and study table, and, encircling the studio, low walnut bookcases with long polished steel hinges.[56]

Here, in this "show-house" and "art-home" the public was told "the genial artist devotes himself to his art." But by 1880 the big house had become an expensive burden, and the unhappy artist wrote his wife, "I detest it, and wish to be rid of it." Creditors forced the sale of house and contents, and in 1885 Cropsey and his family were settled in smaller quarters at Hastings-on-Hudson. The house, which the Cropseys called Ever Rest, had been constructed in the late 1830s as a board-and-batten Gothic Revival cottage similar to those pictured by Downing. Its picturesqueness no doubt appealed to Cropsey, as did the view from the property down a steep slope and west over the broad Hudson to the Palisades.[57]

However much Cropsey came to hate Aladdin, he still brought over to Hastings furniture, several stained-glass windows, and the basic form of his Warwick studio.[58] William Talbot notes that the Hastings house and studio "marked a retrenchment for the artist, and his hopes for some personal peace after the tribulations of 'Aladdin' may be reflected in the name." The artist lived there until his death.[59]

Aladdin and Malkasten are gone. Fortunately their rival, Olana, remains. On July 22, 1872, McEntee, Vaux, and their wives visited Church's summer residence three miles south of the city of Hudson. McEntee recorded the visit in his diary:

> It was a magnificent day. After a nice dinner at his little cottage we went up to his new house which approaches completion. . . . It is certainly a beautiful house and commands one of the finest views of River and Mountain in the country. Church devotes nearly his whole time to building his house, and with his peculiar talent has produced a satisfactory result. The color of the house on the outside by the judicious use of colored bricks with the stone is very harmonious and agreeable. It looks like an artist's work.[60]

5. Richard Morris Hunt (as painted by Frederic E. Church)
COZY COTTAGE FOR FREDERIC E. CHURCH, NEAR HUDSON. c. 1869
Oil sketch, 11½ x 17⅜"
New York State Office of Parks, Recreation and Historic Preservation,
Olana State Historic Site, Hudson, N.Y.

By 1870, when Church began to build the new house (later named Olana), he had traveled widely, yet chose to return to the vicinity of Catskill, where he had lived and studied with Thomas Cole between 1844 and 1846. This was, he wrote his friend Erastus Dow Palmer, "the center of the world." Married in 1860, he bought land the same year and began to build a cottage, completed in 1861, on the slope below the summit where Olana would stand. Designed by Richard Morris Hunt, Cozy Cottage was modest, somewhat reminiscent of Vaux's design for McEntee (see fig. 5).

With the purchase of the summit of the ridge in 1867, Church turned to Hunt for a much grander house. The architect made drawings for both a mansarded château and a Moorish villa, the latter no doubt at Church's request. He had journeyed to the Near East in 1868 and apparently found its exotic, colorful architecture not only paintable but buildable. As McEntee wrote, Olana was truly "an artist's work"—nearly 300 drawings and watercolors for details of the house came from Church's hand (see fig. 6). He was primarily concerned with ornamentally treated features (there are dozens of studies for the main stair banister and numerous alternatives for the slate pattern and cresting of the tower), while he gave his architects some control over matters of space and construction.[61]

Hunt was dismissed; Clive Aslet suggests he was too strong a personality for a client who wanted to create much of the design himself. Instead Church turned to the firm of Vaux, Withers and Co. So it was Vaux who had to adjust to the fact, as Church wrote in 1871, that "I am building a house and am principally my own Architect. I give directions all day and draw plans and working drawings all night."[62]

About 1880 the semi-Arabic name Olana was given to the property by Mrs. Church—perhaps a Latin corruption of the Arabic "Al'ana," or "our place on high." Cropsey's Aladdin had an exotic name not reflected in its architectural style. Olana, on the other hand, was labeled by Mrs. Lamb as "in the Persian style, so far as our climate and requirements permit." In 1871 Church wrote his friend the painter John Ferguson Weir that he had obtained "my architecture from Persia" but admitted he had never actually traveled in Persia, so "I am obliged to imagine Persian architecture." He had some help in these imaginings: Aslet cites books on Persian architecture found in Church's library as sources for some details: the water tower from the "Vue de la Cour de la Mosque Mesdjidi-Chan" in *Monuments de la Perse* by Pascal Coste (Paris, 1867), the piazza columns from more elaborate ones in the "Pavillon des Miroirs" at Isfahan, and some of the stencil patterns for doors from *Les Arts Arabes* by Jules Bourgoin (Paris, 1868). Arabic script was used for decorative borders. The straight-sided pointed arches and richly polychromatic tiles of the exterior were generically Islamic, while the organization of the ground floor—a central court hall opening into all other major rooms—had Persian roots.[63]

There were other influences besides Persian at Olana. Its asymmetrical massing with corner tower resembled a compact Italian villa such as the Edward King villa (1845) in Newport, Rhode Island. The tower roof was French mansarded. The walls of rubble masonry (the stone drawn from the basement excavation) with red brick dressings were comparable to those advocated by Vaux in *Villas and Cottages*. The polychrome (red, black, yellow) bricks and slates had their counterparts in any number of Ruskinian Gothic buildings by Vaux, With-

6. Frederic E. Church
Architectural sketch WINDOW EAST FACADE, OLANA. 1871–72
Watercolor, 14⅞ x 18½"
New York State Office of Parks, Recreation and Historic Preservation, Olana State Historic Site, Hudson, N.Y.

ers, and others.[64] Inside, at least by 1887, were Indian carvings from Lockwood de Forest, a former pupil. The interior was filled with objects from many periods and places, arranged for their visual appeal according to the principles of the Aesthetic movement. One journalist concluded in 1884 that "the whole house is a museum of fine arts, rich in bronzes, paintings, sculptures, and antique and artistic specimens from all over the world." As in the case of Aladdin, light, color, and vistas were carefully manipulated by the artist.[65]

McEntee visited Church in July 1888 and was impressed that, though "much disabled," he retained his "ambition" and was "building a new studio in connection with his house, quite an elaborate building of stone. . . ."[66] Intermittently over the next three years Church, disdainful of any professional architectural advice, made drawings and supervised construction of the studio described by Timothy O'Sullivan as "the last major creative effort of Church's life"—done when a rheumatic wrist ruled out major paintings and when his paintings were no longer fashionable.

Church was well aware that he would probably never be able to make full use of the studio, but the work gave him a chance to be creative in assembling forms, colors, and spaces without taxing his crippled hands. He continued the pointed arches and polychromy of the original house, adding such touches as tiles and buff-colored bricks which O'Sullivan identifies as Mexican, inspired by Church's winter sojourns there in the 1880s.[67]

Just as Church believed in adding touches to his collection of old master paintings to improve them, he felt nature—at least the 250 acres he owned—was susceptible to improvement. Husband and wife laid out a "scatter garden" southeast of the house, but the artist worked on a grander scale in planting thousands of trees in carefully planned patterns. Near the house hemlocks and spruces were planted, "their jagged silhouette complementing its own Picturesque skyline." By 1886 Church had created a lake southwest of the house, which, when viewed from the house, provided a shimmering surface in the midst of trees and led the eye toward the river beyond. He also laid out carriage roads, providing points from which to observe the newly created landscape. Church wrote Palmer in 1884: "I have made about one and three-quarters miles of road this season, opening entirely new and beautiful views—I can make more and better landscapes in this way than by tampering with canvas and paint in the Studio."[68]

Like Bierstadt and Cropsey's studio-houses, Olana was very much the showplace. It was one of the sites to be seen from the decks of Hudson River steamboats; engraved views and descriptions appeared in a variety of publications. No doubt more important to Church was the expectation that the publicity would enhance his reputation as an artist. Roger Stein notes that Church "was a careful promoter of his own work."[69]

George Henry Hall's studio-house, like Olana, stood on a prominent site, and its exterior announced the artist's international experience (fig. 7). Standing very near the road leaving Palenville for the ascent up Kaaterskill Clove, Hall's wooden building had been constructed in the early nineteenth century and served as a store until purchased by the painter in 1871. Hall erected an "ornamental chimney which was long a landmark on the picturesque road, a subject for many an artist's pencil and for every passing photographer. The design was original with Mr. Hall, who brought the tiles that ornamented it from Spain. . . . The hooded windows were suggested to the artist by those he had seen in his extensive European travels." Hall went to Spain in 1860 and 1866, bringing back not only the tiles but furnishings that would be useful props in his many paintings of Spanish themes.[70]

David Maitland Armstrong, painter and stained-glass designer, was a devotee of Italy, studying painting in Rome and serving as consul in the Papal States from 1869 to 1872. Yet when it came to making additions after 1877 to an old farmhouse on family property at Danskammer, on the Hudson north of Newburgh, he would not entertain the idea of an Italian villa; the style was passé. He retained the rambling wooden farmhouse (begun in 1812), but neither he nor his friends and architectural advisers, Charles McKim and Stanford White, appear to have thought its appearance worth extending to the southern additions, which mingled brick and rubble stone ground-story walls (a little like Olana) with an overhanging story of shingles in an American version of the Queen Anne style (fig. 8). The furnishings, Armstrong later confessed, had "too much of the aesthetic" in the choice of tiles (blue-and-white Dutch around the dining-room fireplace) and William Morris

7. R. Lionel De Lisser. GEORGE HENRY HALL STUDIO HOUSE, PALENVILLE
(from PICTURESQUE CATSKILLS, Picturesque Publishing Co.). 1894
Photograph
Courtesy of Alf Evers

8. Helen Maitland Armstrong. DAVID MAITLAND ARMSTRONG STUDIO HOUSE, DANSKAMMER. n.d.
Pencil and watercolor, 18 x 23″
Courtesy of Anne Armstrong Rice

9. R. Lionel De Lisser
WENTWORTH HOUSE INTERIOR, PEEKAMOOSE. 1884
Photograph
Courtesy of Professor and Mrs. William B. Rhoads

wallpapers, but he never lost his faith in the rightness of the "fine old things" brought back from Italy, including a carved chest. The house, according to Armstrong, was "beautifully situated, with a wide view [south] across Newburgh bay to the Highlands." In a second-floor room with large north window he and his daughters Helen and Margaret had a studio where they became increasingly engaged in making stained-glass windows.[71]

George Inness, born on a farm two miles north of Newburgh, shunned the aesthetic studio for what Lizzie Champney called "one of the humblest studios on the Hudson, a certain old barn in an apple orchard in Milton."[72] This served several summers in the early 1880s when Inness boarded with Mrs. Sarah Hull ("Asia") Hallock, whose property was on a bluff overlooking the Hudson. The image of an old barn in an apple orchard was not inconsistent with the pastoral effects Inness achieved in his paintings.

In contrast to the artists discussed thus far, John Quincy Adams Ward sought out a secluded corner of the Catskills in Peekamoose, Ulster County, some nine miles from the nearest railroad station at the hamlet of West Shokan.[73] A sculptor, Ward had no reason to follow the Hudson River School painters by building a towered, hilltop villa. At first he came primarily to fish the headwaters of the Rondout Creek as a member of the tiny (never more than seven members) Peekamoose Fishing Club, which incorporated in 1880 and eventually acquired two thousand acres as a fishing and hunting preserve.[74] Close to a small lake and picturesque gorge a low log cabin was erected with sleeping accommodations for twenty and a fieldstone hearth surmounted by a stone lintel inscribed "The Canty Hearth Where Cronies Meet 1880." Interior walls and doors were "decorated by paintings or carvings by members of the club"—no doubt the carvings (which do not survive) were executed by Ward.[75] The only painter known to have connections with Peekamoose was the Paris-trained portraitist Celia E. Wentworth, but as a woman she was presumably ineligible for club membership.[76] Mrs. Wentworth and her husband, J. W., built a rustic chalet, the Wigwam, near the log clubhouse in 1884 (fig. 9). The name seems to have been justified principally by a painting of an Indian on the chimney-breast.[77] Mrs. Wentworth, a devout Catholic, also had a cliffside chapel erected.

Like Church, Ward was a landscape improver. Annually he built roads, embankments, and bridges to "make the beauties of Peekamoose more accessible without injury to their wildness."[78] About 1885 he altered his keeper's house, a quaint stone cottage of uncertain date, transforming it into a more elaborate "picturesque fishing lodge" for his personal use.[79] (Peekamoose was more than Ward's fishing lodge, for, according to Lewis Sharp, he built a studio there and actively used it.)[80] The half-timbered upper story (purely wooden, without plaster, in the Stick-style manner), trussed and bargeboarded gables, and extravagant dragon heads at the points of the gables may have been intended to evoke medieval Norwegian precedent—fitting, given the steep slope and cascade directly behind the lodge.[81]

Before 1880 artists summered at scattered points in the Hudson Valley, but in the 1880s they began to cluster in colonies in the Catskills. Edward Lamson Henry was the first artist to build on the Shawangunk Ridge above Ellenville and was a founder of the Cragsmoor art colony. In 1883 he purchased land, and the next year his studio-house was under construction, of his own design and built by local carpenter Joseph E. Mance.[82] Henry, a member of the National Academy and an occupant of the 10th Street Studio Building, was drawn to the summit of the Shawangunks by the grandeur of the view (his house had several flat roofs that served as lookouts), but he was also attracted to southern Ulster County by the old-fashioned buildings and people, which he depicted in his widely admired, minutely detailed paintings of historical genre subjects and country life. He collected a wide variety of antique objects to enhance the accuracy of his paintings[83] and also gathered architectural fragments from old houses being demolished in the city, some of which were incorporated into his mountaintop house. The exterior of boards and shingles with ornamental urns, spindles, and balusters attempted to compress many of the features of Queen Anne–style mansions into a house of modest dimen-

10. *Attrib.* Grand Botsford
THE HENRY HOME AT CRAGSMOOR IN HENRY'S TIME. n.d.
Gelatin silver photograph, 5 x 6½"
New York State Museum, Albany, N.Y.

11. Jessie Tarbox Beals. HENRY'S GARDEN. n.d.
Gelatin silver photograph, 7 1/4 x 9 1/2"
New York State Museum, Albany, N.Y.

12. Woodbury and Hunt
E. L. HENRY IN HIS STUDIO AT CRAGSMOOR. n.d.
Gelatin silver photograph, 10 x 8"
New York State Museum, Albany, N.Y.

sions. According to one account, the local carpenters objected that "if you have the rafters show like that . . . and stick the roof all over with little gables, you'll make your studio look like one of them old Dutch manorhouses at Kingston."[84] In fact, the Dutch vernacular of the region was very much simpler than Henry's house, but at the time the Queen Anne style was often believed to be somehow identifiable with old colonial design. Henry's house not only echoed his antiquarian taste in painting subjects but also provided an appropriate setting to inspire his painted re-creations of an earlier America. His use of early American architectural forms was therefore quite different from Charles Herbert Moore's—Henry's being more overtly pictorial and sentimental, Moore's more structural and rational.

In the Northeast the Queen Anne style was gradually transformed in the 1880s into the Shingle style, and this process can be observed at Cragsmoor in comparing Henry's house to some of the slightly later creations of his friend Frederick S. Dellenbaugh. Although no more a professional architect than Henry, Dellenbaugh designed his own house (1891) and others using local stone for lower walls, with shingled upper walls and roof. Bay windows, oriels, dormers, and the contrast of wood and stone made for variety in outline and texture. There was no tacked-on antiquarian detail on his own house, which related nicely to the stone and wood of the mountain: as a student of Indian architecture, Dellenbaugh observed the "moulding effects of the environment . . . in the forms and materials of their dwellings," and as a designer he responded to the setting, as well as to the current vogue for the Shingle style.[85]

As Henry was establishing his summer home on the Shawangunks, Candace Thurber Wheeler was creating her own summer place, the nucleus of Onteora Park, on a hillside in the northern Catskills near Tannersville. Mrs. Wheeler, who had grown up in Delhi in the northwestern Catskills, was well known by 1883 for her efforts in behalf of the revival of artistic needlework (part of her more general interest in improving the economic status of women). She was a close friend of several members of the Hudson River School (Cole, Durand,

Church, Gifford, and McEntee).[86] In the spring of 1883 Candace Wheeler and her brother Francis Thurber went into the Catskills, "looking for some hill from the top of which there would be a great outlook, yet with close and rugged surroundings of trees and rocks and mountains, where we could build a camp or cabin and live the wild life for a little space."

The opening of the Stony Clove and Catskill Mountain Railroad in 1882 had made the high country near Tannersville easily accessible to New York. After detraining, Mrs. Wheeler and her party hired a wagon that eventually brought them up the Eastkill Valley Road to a site near Widow Parker's house, a place hallowed for Mrs. Wheeler by its reputation as a favorite summer abode of Asher Durand. Sister and brother exalted at discovering a pasture from which could be seen "beautiful wooded and rock-piled mountains everywhere . . . with a far-off misty view of miles of the Hudson Valley and beyond the Berkshire Mountains, opalescent and dreamlike." Francis Thurber arranged to buy the farm immediately, and plans were made to build two houses "overlooking the entrancing view."[87]

The two houses built in 1883 were both to be of logs until Mrs. Wheeler learned that logs would be too expensive. She settled for sawed lumber in the construction of her cottage, Pennyroyal, while Thurber pressed forward with his log house. Just as she looked back to early American needlework for inspiration, so, too, she sought to revive the regional vernacular in architecture. In addition to the sentimental appeal of the log cabin, its rustic design would be harmonious with the mountain landscape (see fig. 13).

Built of boards, Pennyroyal (named for the local weed and because "it was so royal and cost but a penny," thought Candace's daughter Dora Wheeler Keith) was put up by local farmers. Its construction was not discordant with the nineteenth-century vernacular of the region. While the house was unpretentious externally, its corner windows with diamond panes and its piazza were both artistic and indicative of the importance of the view for the occupant. The interior was at first dominated by one large, low-ceilinged room with a corner fireplace. Another corner functioned as a library, its windows "looking south and east into a heaven of beauty." The furniture of a summer cottage, Mrs. Wheeler later wrote in *Principles of Home Decoration*, "should be simpler and lighter than in houses intended for constant family living"—and so it was at Pennyroyal, where some of the furniture was made by local carpenters who "developed a real genius for rustic work" (see fig. 8). Mrs. Wheeler added details, especially a grid of flat wood moldings over the ceiling and a frieze of flowers and scroll with motto, that proclaimed the resident designer to be a cultivated exponent of the Aesthetic movement.[88] The plastered east wall was painted (probably by her daughter Dora) with portraits of early visitors, including General George Custer's widow, Libby, the naturalist John Burroughs, and Candace Wheeler's greatest prize, Mark Twain. A simple but apparently dramatic contribution to the room was her choice of curtains made of two layers of cloth, one blue, the other red: "at sunset, when the rays of light are level, the variations are like a sunset sky."

Dora, a pupil of William Merritt Chase, built a studio a few steps east of Pennyroyal. Candace Wheeler described its construction: the "first appearance above ground was . . . a great stone fireplace and chimney, a huge wall of stone with an opening ten feet wide in front to hold long logs which we foresaw turning to fiery iridescence in evenings to come. An inclosure of frame and thick silvery gray slabs in a twenty-five-by-thirty-foot parallelogram surrounded the chimneypiece." While not a true log cabin, the vertical, bark-covered slabs must have been an approximation of Mrs. Wheeler's ideal, so she felt justified in calling it "the log studio."[89]

Pennyroyal and the adjoining studio soon became almost integral parts of the hillside. They reflected Mrs. Wheeler's sensitivity toward nature, which was also indicated by her decision to enclose her flower garden, not with a conventional fence intruding upon the "heavenly slope" flowing from the garden for "fenceless miles" to Kaaterskill Clove and the Hudson Valley, but rather "with a . . . stone-heap . . . not a wall, but a rolling up and circling around of boulders" from the adjacent rocky slope. And the stone wall was made "broad enough to grow weeds and grasses and blossoming stone-crop on its top."[90]

By 1887 the larger community of Onteora Park took form, as Mrs. Wheeler prodded her husband, brother, and two investors to form the Catskill Mountain Camp and Cottage Company. It was her idea to colonize some seven hundred acres of newly acquired land by inviting friends "to come and make homes in our

13. Anonymous EXTERIOR VIEW OF PENNYROYAL. n.d.
Modern print from a 19th-century photograph, 8 x 10"
Courtesy of Onteora Club, N.Y.

paradise." Literary figures, art patrons, and a scattering of artists were prominent among the select list of cottage builders.

J. Carroll Beckwith was the first painter to accept an invitation to build a cottage. Mrs. Wheeler still respected, perhaps even venerated, the memory of the Hudson River School painters: in the 1890s she had the names of Cole, Durand, Church, Gifford, Whittredge, and McEntee carved on Artists' Rock, a natural formation high above Widow Parker's house, to commemorate her "predecessors in love of the Catskills." But by 1890 these men were dead or declining. Candace Wheeler now supported a younger generation of artists such as Beckwith (born 1852), whose broader style her daughter had adopted.

A portrait painter, Beckwith nevertheless chose a site (higher than Pennyroyal's) with an impressive view to the south and Hunter Mountain. The house was built about 1890 (the year Beckwith painted Mark Twain's portrait at Onteora) in the fashionable Shingle style, its porch and broad dormers oriented to the southern panorama. Behind the house Beckwith erected a separate shingled studio in 1906, where he painted portraits of Onteorians and instructed pupils. In the same decade another painter and Wheeler friend, John White Alexander, took over a Shingle-style house just below the Beckwith place and appended a two-story studio space. [91]

14. Candace Wheeler. INTERIOR OF PENNYROYAL
(from *Principles of Home Decoration*,
New York: Doubleday, Page, & Co., 1903)
Photograph, 4⅜ x 5¹¹/₁₆"
Courtesy of a private collection

15. Anonymous. CANDACE WHEELER
IN A GARDEN WITH A YOUNG GIRL. n.d.
Gelatin silver photograph, 3¼ x 3⅝"
Courtesy of Onteora Club, N.Y.

Mrs. Wheeler disapproved of a tendency among cottage owners to demand such luxuries as piped water and bathrooms. Apparently among those who would reject her idea of simple camp and cottage life was the Canadian artist George A. Reid, who is omitted from her lengthy list of Onteorians but was a leading member of its artistic community from 1891 until World War I.[92] Having had some architectural training, Reid was called upon to design cottages as well as the church and library at Onteora; thus he was a rival of Candace Wheeler's son Dunham, an architect who had begun his career at Onteora before Reid's appearance. Reid designed and oversaw construction of his own cottage. His preference for stuccoed exteriors (influenced by British Arts and Crafts cottages) went against the Wheeler-Thurber taste for wood, but the enormous fireplace was akin to the one in Dora Wheeler's studio. Reid's success on his own behalf led to commissions for some twenty cottages in and around Onteora, often with painted friezes, furniture, and hardware designed by him.

Arkville, a hamlet thirty-five miles west of Onteora Park, was the site of a small artists' colony on the lower slope of Pakatakan Mountain. Never so "pretentious" or well known as Onteora, the Pakatakan colony nevertheless attracted a number of significant artists led by J. Francis Murphy and Alexander H. Wyant.[93] Murphy, a disciple of the Barbizon School who saw George Inness as "our greatest man," was the central figure in the development of the colony. According to the account of his wife, artist Adah Clifford Murphy, he urged blacksmith Peter Hoffman to build an inn on the northern base of Pakatakan Mountain, a half mile from the station. The Hoffman House was completed in 1886 and became the focus of the colony's social life. For his part, Murphy encouraged other artists to join him in a summer art colony. In 1887 he bought a lot near the Hoffman House from its proprietor and constructed a small cottage[94] (figs. 16–19).

Sketches for the building had been drawn by New York architect Charles T. Mott: fieldstone walls emerged from the sloping hillside; roof and gables were shingled; generous porches faced east and west, and the high north elevation was distinguished by a studio window (fig. 19). As built, the stonework was reduced in

17. Anonymous
MRS. J. FRANCIS MURPHY
AT WEEDWILD. c. 1890
Gelatin silver photograph, 9¼ x 7½"
Emerson Crosby Kelly Papers,
Archives of American Art,
Smithsonian Institution, Washington, D.C.

16. Anonymous MR. AND MRS. J. FRANCIS MURPHY
IN FRONT OF THEIR FIRST HOUSE AT ARKVILLE, N.Y.
c. 1890. Albumen silver photograph, 4⅜ x 3¾"
Emerson Crosby Kelly Papers, Archives of American Art,
Smithsonian Institution, Washington, D.C.

favor of shingling, and the large cross gable was cut down to a shed dormer. The resulting simple Shingle-style cottage signified the spread to the western Catskills of the unassuming wooden architecture then in vogue at Onteora and countless other summer resorts.[95] The cottage's name, Weedwild, befitted both its unglamorous design and the owner's preference for common plants and wildflowers (as was true of Pennyroyal and Candace Wheeler). Murphy did not paint outdoors and did little sketching at Arkville. His life outside, as he confessed to dealer William Macbeth on July 22, 1892, involved "a good long time with hoe and rake. . . . I have not unpacked my colors yet. . . . [My] garden is now my palette."[96]

Weedwild's interior had studios for husband and wife but no kitchen—meals were taken at the Hoffman House. The architectural treatment of the rooms was very plain, except for the angled fireplaces, but the artists added standard studio bric-a-brac: a pensive Adah Murphy was photographed in a colonial rocker while an idle spinning wheel and mandolin decorated the hearth.

The simplicity of the architecture and garden was influenced by Murphy's admiration of Henry David Thoreau's admittedly much more primitive hut at Walden Pond, which he visited in 1882 and again in 1919 when he collected pine seedlings and transplanted them at the Arkville studio. The old vernacular buildings around Arkville and their unregimented settings appeared in several Murphy sketches and canvases and must have had an effect on his planning.[97] In subsequent years a prosperous Murphy bought adjoining mountain land and added structures in harmony with the original cottage. In 1899 a house was built a few yards up the hill from the first cottage, with Arkville builder Scudder Whipple probably working from Murphy's own Shingle-style design.[98]

Alexander Wyant and his wife, Arabella (also a painter), had occupied a summer house in the Adirondacks at Keene Valley since 1875, but in 1887 they, too, arrived at the Hoffman House. After unpacking, Mrs. Wyant noted in her diary that they "strolled through the woods to a little log cabin that is to be Aleck's

18. Anonymous
FIRST MURPHY HOUSE
AT ARKVILLE, N.Y. c. 1890
Albumen silver photograph, 7⅞ x 9⅜″
Emerson Crosby Kelly Papers,
Archives of American Art,
Smithsonian Institution, Washington, D.C.

19. Charles T. Mott
PROPOSED J. FRANCIS MURPHY COTTAGE, ARKVILLE.
c. 1887 Photo reproduction, 9¼ x 14″
Emerson Crosby Kelly Papers, Archives of American Art,
Smithsonian Institution, Washington, D.C.

20. Alexander H. Wyant. ARKVILLE LANDSCAPE. n.d.
Oil on canvas, 16¼ x 24¼"
Cleveland Museum of Art.
The Charles W. Harkness Gift

studio—the country is beautiful, but it is not the Adirondacks, and I miss Keene Valley, and our little house there . . . but Aleck thinks he will find what he wants here. . . ." Wyant expanded the log cabin with a porch and a room for his wife. Within two weeks Mrs. Wyant observed that "our shanty is finished and very cozy, with its hammock and big easy chairs, and with a few rugs we brought looks quite homelike." The Murphys, the Kruseman Van Eltens, the Charles Smillies, and several of Helen Smillie's pupils were "dotted here and there through the woods, we make quite a little artistic community."[99]

The Wyant shanty was supplanted in 1889 by a fine Shingle-style house, its south elevation suggesting a broad triangle like Charles McKim's Low house (1886–87) in Bristol, Rhode Island. Yet Wyant, like Murphy, probably believed that his shingled house was linked to local tradition, which he portrayed in such paintings as *Old House near Arkville*. Neither Wyant nor Murphy chose to build on very high sites with dramatic vistas such as appealed to Bierstadt and Church. As Tonalists, both were drawn to the quieter, more intimate aspects of the landscape.[100]

Where Wyant's substantial contemporary reputation was mirrored in the large scale of his summer house,[101] Edward L. Field's very modest place among American landscape painters and illustrators was suggested by his diminutive studio cottage called Edsden, built in 1889. Another example of the Shingle style, it was clearly defined as a studio by the window dominating the north wall. An early pen-and-ink perspective by Field shows the rustic porch posts were tree trunks or limbs.

Arkville's art colony was by 1891 something of a tourist attraction. As Hudson River guidebooks alerted steamboat passengers to the splendor of Olana, so the guide to the Catskills put out by the Ulster and Delaware Railroad advised passengers that "several very attractive summer cottages . . . many of them [built] by artists of note . . . may be seen . . . peering through the trees on the mountain slope."[102]

21. *Attrib.* Jessie Tarbox Beals
WHITE PINES, RALPH RADCLIFFE WHITEHEAD STUDIO HOUSE, BYRDCLIFFE, WOODSTOCK. 1902
Photograph, 5 x 7″
Mr. and Mrs. Mark Willcox

22. E. Loyal Field. EDSDEN. 1897
Watercolor, 5 x 8″
Courtesy of Alice Zigelis

23. Anonymous
E. L. FIELD SKETCHING AT PAKATAKAN.
n.d. Cyanotype, 4¼ x 3¼″
Courtesy of a private collection

By the turn of the century the Catskills were not only well trod but also well inhabited by artists. It is therefore hardly surprising that in 1902, when Ralph Radcliffe Whitehead and Bolton Brown were selecting a site for an art colony, they chose Woodstock in the Catskills. Like his predecessors at Onteora, Whitehead built his own house (fig. 21) to overlook "an immense range of mountain and valley" and treated the woodwork inside and out so that it "appears to have grown out of its happy environment."[103]

1. Len Jenshel
VIEW FROM THE HARVEY PROPERTY, HASTINGS-ON-HUDSON, N.Y.

2. Len Jenshel
HOUSE ON ORIGINAL HARVEY PROPERTY
(GARDENER'S COTTAGE)

3. George Harvey. AFTERNOON—HASTINGS LANDING, PALISADES ROCKS IN SHADOW, N.Y. c. 1836
Watercolor, 8⅜ x 13⅝"
New-York Historical Society, N.Y.
Gift of Mrs. Screven Lorillard, 1952

4. Robert W. Weir
VIEW OF THE HUDSON RIVER FROM WEST POINT. n.d.
Oil on canvas, 13 x 21″
Putnam County Historical Society,
Cold Spring, N.Y.

6. Len Jenshel
VIEW OF THE HUDSON AT WEST POINT

5. Seth Eastman
VIEW OF WEST POINT. c. 1845
Oil on canvas, 6½ x 9″
West Point Museum Collections,
United States Military Academy, West Point, N.Y.

7. John Ferguson Weir
THE ARTIST'S STUDIO. 1864
Oil on canvas, 15¼ x 12¼"
Yale University Art Gallery, New Haven, Conn. Gift of Mr. and Mrs. Russell C. Graef

8. John Ferguson Weir
INTERIOR OF HIS FATHER'S QUARTERS AT WEST POINT. 1867
Oil on canvas, 10½ x 15¾"
Courtesy of the Reverend and Mrs. DeWolf Perry

9. E. L. Henry. WEST POINT FROM PROFESSOR WEIR'S. n.d.
Pencil on paper, 5 x 8½"
New York State Museum, Albany, N.Y.

10. Len Jenshel
ENTRANCE TO THE THOMAS COLE HOUSE,
CATSKILL, N.Y.

11. Charles Herbert Moore
THOMAS COLE'S HOUSE ("CEDAR GROVE"). 1868
Oil on canvas mounted on board, 6 x 9¼″
Courtesy of Edith Cole Silberstein

12. Charles Herbert Moore
THOMAS COLE'S FIRST STUDIO. 1862
Oil on canvas mounted on board, 8 x 11½″
Courtesy of Edith Cole Silberstein

13. *Attrib.* Thomas Cole. POINT MERINO. c. 1837. Oil on canvas, 33⅛ x 44⅛″
Parrish Art Museum, Southampton, N.Y. The Littlejohn Collection

14. Jasper F. Cropsey
THOMAS COLE'S STUDIO, CATSKILL, N.Y.
(THE SECOND STUDIO).
c. 1850. Pencil on paper, 3⅜ x 4⅞″
Wadsworth Atheneum, Hartford, Conn.

15. Thomas C. Farrar
A BUCKWHEAT FIELD ON THOMAS COLE'S FARM
1863. Oil on canvas, 11¾ x 25″
Museum of Fine Arts, Boston.
Gift of Maxim Karolik to the M. and M. Karolik Collection
of American Paintings, 1962

16. Len Jenshel
INTERIOR OF THE THOMAS COLE HOUSE, CATSKILL, N.Y.

17. Len Jenshel
EXTERIOR VIEW OF THE THOMAS COLE HOUSE,
CATSKILL, N.Y.

107

18. John Henry Hill. OLD HILL STUDIO, WEST NYACK. 1870
Watercolor, 12 x 12½″
New-York Historical Society. Gift of The Adirondack Museum, 1956

19. Len Jenshel
EXTERIOR OF THE JOHN WILLIAM HILL HOUSE

"CONSIDER THE LILIES"—JOHN W. HILL'S HOMESTEAD.

21. Anonymous. "CONSIDER THE LILLIES"
—JOHN W. HILL'S HOMESTEAD
"Fac-simile of drawing after a watercolor by J. W. Hill"
From *Harper's Magazine*, vol. 80, 1889–90, 3 x 3½″
Vassar College Library, Poughkeepsie, N.Y.

20. Len Jenshel
EXTERIOR OF THE HILL HOMESTEAD

22. Robert Havell, Jr.

VIEW OF THE HUDSON RIVER FROM NEAR SING SING. c. 1850. Oil on canvas, 36 x 50″

(Inscribed on verso, "View of the Hudson River Tappan Bay, taken from Rocky Mount near Sing Sing")

New-York Historical Society. John Jay Watson Fund, 1971

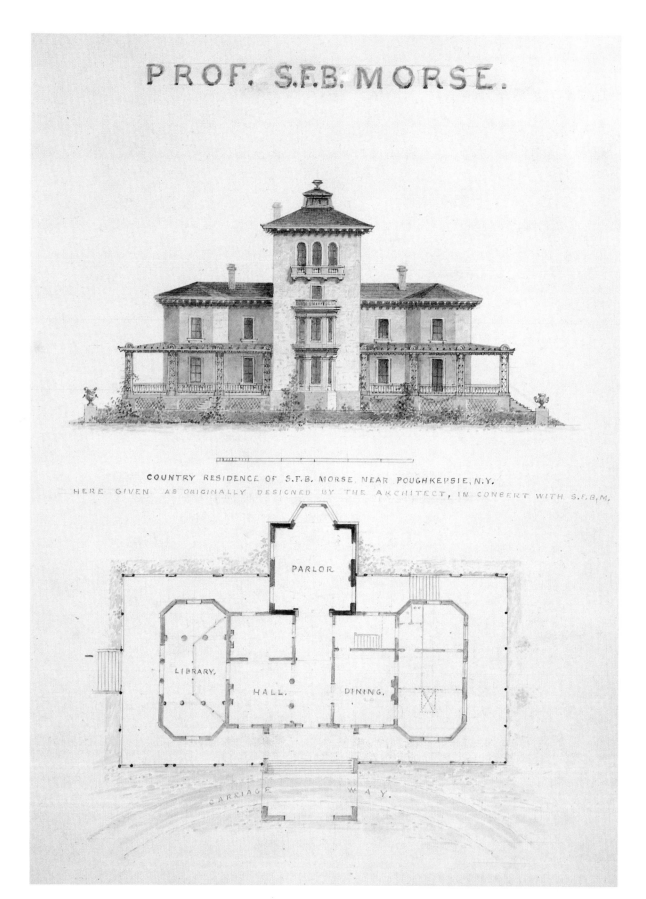

PROF. S.F.B. MORSE.

COUNTRY RESIDENCE OF S.F.B. MORSE, NEAR POUGHKEPSIE, N.Y.
HERE GIVEN AS ORIGINALLY DESIGNED BY THE ARCHITECT, IN CONBERT WITH S.F.B.M.

PARLOR

LIBRARY.

HALL.

DINING.

CARRIAGE WAY.

23. Alexander Jackson Davis
COUNTRY RESIDENCE OF S. F. B. MORSE, NEAR POUGHKEEPSIE, N.Y.
RIVERFRONT ELEVATION AND PLANS. n.d.
Watercolor, 17¼ x 13½″
From a book of Davis designs, *Rural Residences* portfolio, 24.66.1416 (18)
The Metropolitan Museum of Art, New York.
Harris Brisbane Dick Fund. 1924 (24.66.1416[17])

24. Slee Brothers. MORSE HOUSE WITH MEMBERS OF THE MORSE FAMILY. c. 1870
Albumen silver photograph, 10⅜ x 14″
Young-Morse Historic Site, Poughkeepsie, N.Y.

25. Len Jenshel
THE PORCH OF THE SAMUEL F. B. MORSE HOUSE,
LOCUST GROVE, WITH PATH LEADING TO THE RIVER,
POUGHKEEPSIE, N.Y.

26. Len Jenshel
EXTERIOR VIEW OF LOCUST GROVE,
POUGHKEEPSIE, N.Y.

DESIGN FOR AN ARTIST'S STUDIO.

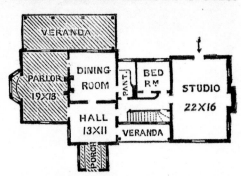

PLAN OF PRINCIPAL FLOOR.

N.E. VIEW.

SHOWING THE COTTAGE COMPLETED.

27. Calvert Vaux

DESIGN FOR AN ARTIST'S STUDIO (JERVIS McENTEE'S STUDIO IN RONDOUT). 1864

From Vaux, *Villas and Cottages*, New York: Harper and Brothers, p. 168

Vassar College Library, Poughkeepsie, N.Y.

28. Jervis McEntee
VIEW FROM THE STUDIO WINDOW. n.d.
Oil on canvas, 6⅜ x 11½″
Courtesy of Mr. and Mrs. Herbert L. Shultz

29. Jervis McEntee
LANDSCAPE VIEW FACING THE CATSKILL MOUNTAINS
1863. Oil on canvas, 16⅛ x 32″
Courtesy of a private collection

30. Len Jenshel
PORCH AT ROSSITER HOUSE, COLD SPRING, N.Y.

31. Thomas P. Rossiter
THE HUDSON FROM HIS HOUSE AT COLD SPRING
n.d. Oil on canvas, 6 x 9¼″
Julia L. Butterfield Memorial Library, Cold Spring, N.Y.

32. Thomas P. Rossiter. ROSSITER FAMILY ON
THE PIAZZA OF HIS HOUSE IN COLD SPRING. 1862
Oil on canvas, 28 x 45″
Courtesy of Theodore Kensett Rossiter

33. Len Jenshel. EXTERIOR OF THOMAS P. ROSSITER'S HOUSE
WITH VIEW TO RIVER, COLD SPRING, N.Y.

34. Frederic E. Church
VIEW OF OLANA FROM THE SOUTHWEST. c. 1875–80
Pencil and oil on cardboard, 12⅛ x 9½″
Cooper-Hewitt Museum
Smithsonian Institution/Art Resource, New York

35. *Attrib.* Frederic E. Church
ARCHITECTURAL DRAWING OF OLANA, SOUTHWEST ELEVATION.
c. 1870 Pencil and watercolor, 13 x 21¹⁵/₁₆″
New York State Office of Parks, Recreation and
Historic Preservation, Olana State Historic Site, Hudson, N.Y.

36. Len Jenshel. EXTERIOR OF OLANA

37. Len Jenshel. INTERIOR OF OLANA LOOKING THROUGH TO PORCH, HUDSON, N.Y.

38. Len Jenshel
INTERIOR DETAIL AT OLANA, HUDSON, N.Y.

39. Len Jenshel
VIEW FROM THE GARDEN AT OLANA, HUDSON, NY.

40. Frederic E. Church
NIGHTFALL NEAR OLANA. 1872
Oil on canvas, 9½ x 14⅛"
Cooper-Hewitt Museum,
Smithsonian Institution/Art Resource, New York

41. Len Jenshel
VIEW TOWARD HUDSON RIVER FROM THE PORCH AT OLANA,
HOUSE OF FREDERIC E. CHURCH, HUDSON, N.Y.

42. Charles Herbert Moore
THE CATSKILLS IN SPRING. 1861
Oil on canvas, 12⅛ x 20⅜"
Vassar College Art Gallery, Poughkeepsie, N.Y.
Gift of Matthew Vassar

43. Len Jenshel
EXTERIOR VIEW
OF THE CHARLES HERBERT MOORE HOUSE,
ORIGINAL WING DESIGNED BY MOORE,
CATSKILL, N.Y.

44. Len Jenshel
VIEW OF HUDSON LOOKING TOWARD OLANA
FROM THE ROOF OF THE CHARLES HERBERT MOORE HOUSE,
CATSKILL, N.Y.

45. Arthur Parton
LOOKING SOUTHWEST OVER CHURCH'S FARM FROM THE SIENGHENBERGH. 1864
Oil on canvas, 12⅞ x 24¼″
New York State Office of Parks, Recreation and
Historic Preservation, Olana State Historic Site, Hudson, N.Y.

46. Charles Herbert Moore
WINTER LANDSCAPE, VALLEY OF THE CATSKILLS. 1866
Oil on canvas, 7 x 10″
Art Museum, Princeton University.
Gift of Frank Jewett Mather, Jr.

47. Len Jenshel
FIREPLACE WITH DECORATIVE TILEWORK,
CHARLES HERBERT MOORE HOUSE,
CATSKILL, N.Y.

48. Walter Launt Palmer
HOUSE AT VAN WIES' POINT. 1898
Pencil and wash on paper, 7⅞ x 10⅝″
Albany Institute of History and Art, N.Y.

49. F. J. Haines
STEREO VIEW OF APPLEDALE. 1870–80
Albumen silver photographs on stereo card, image, 3 x 3″
Albany Institute of History and Art, N.Y.

50. Walter Launt Palmer
THE DINING ROOM AT APPLEDALE. 1877
Oil on canvas, 25 x 20″
Albany Institute of History and Art, N.Y.
Bequest of Robert W. Olcott

51. Albert Bierstadt
ON THE HUDSON NEAR IRVINGTON. n.d.
Oil on board, 7¼ x 12¼"
Berkshire Museum, Pittsfield, Mass.
Gift of Miss Mabel Choate

52. Charles Bierstadt
INTERIOR AT MALKASTEN. c. 1870
Albumen silver photographs
on stereo card, image, 4 x 3"
Courtesy of Joyce Randall Edwards

53. Sanford R. Gifford
MT. MERINO. 1859
Oil on canvas, 7½ x 15½"
Courtesy 1987 Sotheby's, Inc., New York

54. E. W. Cook
SANFORD GIFFORD'S STUDIO BELVEDERE. n.d.
Albumen silver photograph, image, 4 x 6"
New York State Library, Albany, N.Y.

55. Sanford R. Gifford. MARSHES ON THE HUDSON. 1878
Oil on canvas, 16½ x 30¼"
Courtesy of Thomas Coleville Fine Art, Inc., New Haven, Conn.

56. D. Maitland Armstrong
CHIMNEY CORNER. 1878
Oil on canvas, 21½ x 16½″
Collection of Kingscote
Preservation Society
of Newport County, Newport, R.I.

57. Anonymous
INTERIOR OF ARMSTRONG HOUSE,
DINING ROOM SIDEBOARD. 1890
Modern print of a 19th-century photograph,
4¼ x 7½″
Courtesy of Anne Armstrong Rice

58. Helen Maitland Armstrong
INTERIOR VIEW OF THE ARMSTRONG HOUSE. n.d.
Watercolor, 12¾ x 9″
Courtesy of Anne Armstrong Rice

59. Len Jenshel
GEORGE INNESS'S STUDIO BARN, MILTON, N.Y.

60. George Inness. OVERLOOKING THE HUDSON AT MILTON. 1888

Oil on canvas, 21³⁄₈ x 16½"

Nelson-Atkins Museum of Art, Kansas City (Nelson Fund)

61. Len Jenshel
THE CROPSEY HOUSE, EVER REST,
AT HASTINGS-ON-HUDSON, N.Y.

63. Jasper F. Cropsey
INTERIOR OF THE STUDIO AT WARWICK, N.Y. 1876
Watercolor and pencil, 11 x 11"
Newington-Cropsey Foundation,
Hastings-on-Hudson, N.Y.

Opposite:
65. Jasper F. Cropsey
A VIEW FROM THE ARTIST'S RESIDENCE,
HASTINGS-UPON-HUDSON, N.Y. 1890
Watercolor, 7¼ x 4¼"
Newington-Cropsey Foundation,
Hastings-on-Hudson, N.Y.

62. Len Jenshel.
INTERIOR OF THE CROPSEY STUDIO,
SHOWING THE INGLENOOK,
HASTINGS-ON-HUDSON, N.Y.

64. Len Jenshel
INTERIOR OF THE CROPSEY HOUSE, SHOWING
THE STAINED GLASS HE DESIGNED FOR ALADDIN
AND INCORPORATED IN THE SECOND HOUSE,
HASTINGS-ON-HUDSON, N.Y.

J.F. Cropsey 1890.

A View from the Artist
Residence.
Hastings-upon-Hudson. N.Y.

67. Len Jenshel
THE ROBERT FULTON LUDLOW HOUSE,
EXTERIOR VIEW, CLAVERACK, N.Y.

66. Robert Fulton Ludlow
WOMAN FROM THE LUDLOW FAMILY
WITH HOLLYHOCKS. c. 1880–90
Modern print from a 19th-century glass negative, 8 x 10″
Columbia County Historical Society,
Kinderhook, N.Y.

68. Len Jenshel
E. L. HENRY'S STUDIO, CRAGSMOOR, N.Y.

69. Len Jenshel
INTERIOR OF THE E. L. HENRY HOUSE
WITH COLONIAL INSPIRED MANTELPIECE
AND ORIGINAL WALL PAINTING,
CRAGSMOOR, N.Y.

70. E. L. Henry. VESPERS. 1898.
Oil on canvas, 15 x 25"
Courtesy of Fred Radl

72. E. L. Henry
THE HENRY HOUSE AT CRAGSMOOR. 1892
Oil on wood panel, 8½ x 9½"
New York State Museum, Albany, N.Y.

71. E. L. Henry
ORCHARD AND GROUNDS AT THE E. L. HENRY HOUSE
n.d. Gelatin silver photograph, 11 x 14"
New York State Museum, Albany, N.Y.

73. Frederick Dellenbaugh.
FIRE ON THE MOUNTAIN. 1881
Watercolor, 5³⁄₈ x 8³⁄₈"
New York State Museum, Albany, N.Y.

75. Anonymous
INTERIOR AT ENDRIDGE. c. 1910
Gelatin silver photograph, 7 x 9"
New York Public Library, Astor, Lenox,
and Tilden Foundations, Manuscripts Division

74. Len Jenshel
FREDERICK DELLENBAUGH'S HOUSE, ENDRIDGE,
AT CRAGSMOOR, N.Y.

76. Len Jenshel
EXTERIOR VIEW OF THE MAIN HOUSE
AT CHETOLAH, CRAGSMOOR, N.Y.

77. Len Jenshel
INTERIOR VIEW OF THE MAIN HOUSE
AT CHETOLAH, CRAGSMOOR, N.Y.

78. Anonymous
SALE CATALOGUE OF CHETOLAH,
DESIGNED BY GEORGE INNESS, JR.,
AND HOWARD GREENELY. 1927 10 x 6¾"
Courtesy of Kaycee Benton Parra

79. Len Jenshel
18TH-CENTURY STRUCTURE ON THE ELIZA GREATOREX
PROPERTY, CHETOLAH, AT CRAGSMOOR, N.Y.
(PROPERTY LATER SOLD TO GEORGE INNESS, JR.)

80. Len Jenshel
GARDEN DETAIL, CHETOLAH, CRAGSMOOR, N.Y.

81. Len Jenshel
GATE, GEORGE INNESS, JR., PROPERTY, CHETOLAH, CRAGSMOOR, N.Y.

82. Dora Wheeler Keith

PORTRAIT OF CANDACE WHEELER AT ONTEORA PARK. n.d.

Oil on canvas, 7 x 5′

Courtesy of Onteora Club, N.Y.

83. Len Jenshel
INTERIOR AT PENNYROYAL WITH PAINTED DECORATIONS UNDER THE CEILING

84. Len Jenshel
PENNYROYAL, CANDACE WHEELER'S HOUSE, WITH ADJACENT STUDIO
USED BY HER DAUGHTER, DORA WHEELER KEITH, EXTERIOR.

85. Len Jenshel
ALL SOULS' CHURCH,
DESIGNED BY GEORGE REID,
ONTEORA PARK, N.Y.

86. George L. Reid
VIEW FROM THE ARTIST'S SEAT.
1902. Pastel on paper, 30 x 16"
Courtesy of Onteora Club, N.Y.

88. Len Jenshel
GEORGE REID HOUSE, INTERIOR,
NEAR TANNERSVILLE, N.Y.

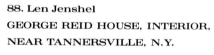

87. Len Jenshel
THE BECKWITH HOUSE, FACING SOUTH,
ONTEORA PARK, N.Y.

89. J. Carroll Beckwith
LANDSCAPE (FROM ARTIST'S SEAT). 1895
Oil on canvas, 19 x 16″
Courtesy of Onteora Club, N.Y.

90. Len Jenshel
INTERIOR OF JOHN QUINCY ADAMS WARD'S COTTAGE,
PROBABLY HIS STUDIO, PEEKAMOOSE MOUNTAIN, N.Y.

91. Len Jenshel
CELIA WENTWORTH'S RUSTIC CHAPEL,
PEEKAMOOSE MOUNTAIN, N.Y.

92. Len Jenshel
GARDEN POOL AT PEEKAMOOSE MOUNTAIN, N.Y.

93. Parker Mann. THE WYANT HOUSE. n.d.
Oil on canvas, 11¾ x 15¾"
Courtesy of Mr. and Mrs. Verne Vance

94. Anonymous
FAMILY AND FRIENDS ON THE WYANT PORCH
From an album of photographs c. 1895
Gelatin silver photograph, sheet, 5½ x 7"
Courtesy of a private collection

95. Anonymous
INTERIOR OF THE WYANT HOUSE. n.d.
Gelatin silver photograph, 5⅝ x 3¼"
Courtesy of a private collection

96. Len Jenshel
J. FRANCIS MURPHY HOUSE,
PAKATAKAN COLONY, ARKVILLE, N.Y.

97. Len Jenshel
J. FRANCIS MURPHY SUMMER STUDIO BUILDING,
PAKATAKAN COLONY, ARKVILLE, N.Y.

98. J. Francis Murphy
THE LONE TREE, ARKVILLE. n.d.
Oil on canvas, 11 x 15½"
Courtesy of Mr. and Mrs. Herbert Baer Brill

99. Len Jenshel. J. FRANCIS MURPHY GARDEN,
SUMMER STUDIO BUILDING,
PAKATAKAN COLONY, ARKVILLE, N.Y.

100. Len Jenshel
J. FRANCIS MURPHY BARN STUDIO, PAKATAKAN,
PAKATAKAN COLONY, ARKVILLE, N.Y.

101. Len Jenshel STUDIO ENTRANCE WITH
WROUGHT IRON HINGES AND DOOR PLATE
DESIGNED BY THE ARTIST, PARKER MANN.
PAKATAKAN COLONY, ARKVILLE, N.Y.

102. Len Jenshel. PARKER MANN STUDIO WING,
PAKATAKAN COLONY, ARKVILLE, N.Y.

103. Len Jenshel
LOYAL FIELD HOUSE, STUDIO WINDOW,
PAKATAKAN, ARKVILLE, N.Y.

104. Len Jenshel. THE LOCKE HOUSE
(ARABELLA WYANT'S SISTER'S HOUSE)
AT PAKATAKAN COLONY, ARKVILLE, N.Y.

105. Len Jenshel
INTERIOR OF THE PARKER MANN HOUSE,
PAKATAKAN COLONY, ARKVILLE, N.Y.

106. J. H. Moser
INTERIOR OF MANN HOUSE, ARKVILLE, N.Y. 1890
Watercolor, 14 x 19"
Courtesy of Mr. and Mrs. Verne Vance

144

Notes

Chapter 1

I am grateful to the following persons for their assistance in the preparation of this essay: Sandra Phillips, curator of the exhibition; Milton W. Brown, Professor of Art History Emeritus, Graduate Center, City University of New York; James M. Fitch, Professor of Architecture Emeritus, Columbia University; Harvey K. Flad, Professor of Geography, Vassar College; Elliott S. M. Gatner, Professor of History Emeritus, Long Island University; Milton M. Klein, Lindsay Young Distinguished Professor Emeritus, University of Tennessee; and Linda Weintraub, director of the Edith C. Blum Art Institute, Bard College Center.

As curator of an exhibition concerned with existing buildings and landscapes within a special location, Dr. Phillips sought to impart her sense of the places discussed. Together we visited the still intact settlement of what had been the art colony of Pakatakan, at Arkville. And through her introduction I visited selected sites in Poughkeepsie, including the summer home of Samuel F. B. Morse, Locust Grove, now known as the Young-Morse Historic Site. The Young family bought the place in 1901 and later endowed it as a private historic property. I am indebted to Timothy Countryman, manager of the site, for a most informative tour of the house and grounds.

Linda Weintraub and her associate, Elaine Ring, worked diligently to obtain the illustrations for the essay. Most of all, I am grateful to my wife, Sandra Friedman Fein, whose keen editorial eye has read and reviewed every word in this essay.

Albert Fein
Brooklyn Campus,
Long Island University
October 1987

---

1. The significance of this tension in American civilization has been illuminated by Henry Nash Smith, *Virgin Land: The American West as Symbol and Myth* (Cambridge, Mass.: Harvard Univ. Press, 1950); Hans Huth, *Nature and the American: Three Centuries of Changing Attitudes* (Berkeley, Calif.: Univ. of Calif. Press, 1957; Lincoln, Neb.: Univ. of Nebraska Press, 1972); Charles L. Sanford, *The Quest for Paradise, Europe and the American Moral Imagination* (Urbana, Ill.: Univ. of Ill. Press, 1961); Leo Marx, *The Machine in the Garden: Technology and the Pastoral Ideal in America* (New York: Oxford Univ. Press, 1964); Roderick Nash, *Wilderness and the American Mind* (New Haven: Yale Univ. Press, 1967); David W. Noble, *The Eternal Adam and the New World Garden: The Central Myth in the American Novel Since 1830* (New York: George Braziller, 1968); John F. Kasson, *Civilizing the Machine: Technology and Republican Values in America, 1776–1900* (New York: Penguin, 1977); and Howard P. Segal, *Technological Utopianism in American Culture* (Chicago: Univ. of Chicago Press, 1985).

2. The impact of the steam ferry on the Hudson River Valley is discussed in Benson J. Lossing, *The Empire State: A Compendious History of the Commonwealth of New York* (New York: American Publishing, 1888), as well as in his self-illustrated *The Hudson from the Wilderness to the Sea* (New York: Virtue, 1866; reprinted Kennikat Press, 1972). The story of the building of the Erie Canal is well told in Ronald E. Shaw, *Erie Water West: A History of the Erie Canal, 1792–1854* (Lexington, Kty.: Univ. of Kentucky Press, 1966); for the larger economic significance of the Erie Canal, see Carter Goodrich, *Government Promotion of American Canals and Railroads, 1800–1890* (New York: Columbia Univ. Press, 1960); Goodrich et al, *Canals and American Economic Development* (New York: Columbia Univ. Press, 1961); and Robert G. Albion, *The Rise of New York Port, 1815–1860* (New York: Charles Scribner's Sons, 1939). The books by Goodrich and Albion also contribute to an understanding of the regional impact of the railroad, a topic central to Carl W. Condit, *The Port of New York: A History of the Rail and Terminal System from the Beginning to Pennsylvania Station* (Chicago: Univ. of Chicago Press, 1980). For the introduction of water into New York City, see Nelson M. Blake, *Water for the Cities* (Syracuse, N.Y.: Syracuse Univ. Press, 1956).

Among the books assessing the significance of the Hudson River School are James Thomas Flexner, *That Wilder Image: The Painting of America's Native School from Thomas Cole to Winslow Homer* (Boston: Bonanza Books, 1962); Neil Harris, *The Artist in American Society: The Formative Years, 1790–1860* (New York: George Braziller, 1966); Barbara Novak, *American Painting of the Nineteenth Century: Realism, Idealism, and the American Experience* (New York: Praeger, 1969); John K. Howat, *The Hudson River and Its Painters* (New York: Viking, 1972); Raymond J. O'Brien, *American Sublime: Landscape and Scenery of the Lower Hudson Valley* (New York: Columbia Univ. Press, 1981); and John K. Howat et al, *American Paradise: The World of the Hudson River School* (New York: Metropolitan Museum of Art, 1987).

3. This regional integrity is reflected in the life and work of Benson J. Lossing, a resident historian-artist of the Hudson River Valley. For an exceptional description of the aesthetics of the Valley see Walter L. Creese, *The Crowning of the American Landscape: Eight Great Spaces and Their Buildings* (Princeton: Princeton Univ. Press, 1985), pp. 43–98.

4. For a discussion of the transition of landscape gardening to landscape architecture, see Laura W. Roper, *FLO: A Biography of Frederick Law Olmsted* (Baltimore: Johns Hopkins Univ. Press, 1973), pp. 143–44; April 1860 is noted as the date "Olmsted and Vaux [were] appointed 'Landscape Architects and designers to the Commissioners North of 155th

Street' " in Frederick Law Olmsted, Jr., and Theodora Kimball, eds., *Forty Years of Landscape Architecture* I (New York: G. P. Putnam's Sons, 1922), p. 8; also, Charles C. McLaughlin, ed., *The Papers of Frederick Law Olmsted* (Baltimore: Johns Hopkins Univ. Press, 1983), III: *Creating Central Park, 1857–1861,* Charles E. Beveridge and David Schuyler, eds., p. 267. The relationship of landscape architecture to art, science, and technology is a theme addressed in Roper, *FLO;* Elizabeth Stevenson, *Park Maker: A Life of Frederick Law Olmsted* (New York: Macmillan, 1977); Albert Fein, *Frederick Law Olmsted and the American Environmental Tradition* (New York: George Braziller, 1972); Albert Fein, "History Section," in *The First Historic Landscape Report for the Ravine, Prospect Park, Brooklyn, New York* (New York: Walmsley & Company, 1986), pp. 1–79. For Olmsted's views on the interrelation of landscape architecture and the growth of cities as regional centers, see his essay *Public Parks and the Enlargement of Towns* (printed for the American Social Science Association, Cambridge, Mass.: Riverside Press, 1870).

5. For discussions of the significance of Downing's influence, see Harris, *The Artist in American Society,* pp. 208–16, 380–83; David Handlin, *The American Home: Architecture and Society, 1815–1915* (Boston: Little, Brown, 1979), pp. 34–48; Francis R. Kowsky, *The Architecture of Frederick Clarke Withers and the Progress of the Gothic Revival in America after 1850* (Middletown, Conn.: Wesleyan Univ. Press, 1980), pp. 8–11; and Creese, pp. 43–98. For biographical details concerning Downing, see Handlin, pp. 41–42.

6. Andrew Jackson Downing, *A Treatise on the Theory and Practice of Landscape Gardening Adapted to North America; with a View to the Improvement of Country Residences,* 6th ed. (New York: C. M. Saxton, Barker & Co., 1860), p. 22. The article describing Birkenhead Park is Frederick Law Olmsted, "The People's Park at Birkenhead, near Liverpool," *Horticulturist* (May 1851), pp. 224–28.

7. Downing, *A Treatise on the Theory and Practice of Landscape Gardening,* pp. viii–ix.

8. For an analysis of Downing's contributions to a theory of domestic architecture, see Handlin, *The American Home,* and Kowsky, *The Architecture of Frederick Clarke Withers;* for a discussion of the development of tourism in the first third of the nineteenth century, including the origin of the Catskill Mountain House, see Huth, *Nature and the American,* Chap. 5.

9. Downing, *A Treatise on the Theory and Practice of Landscape Gardening,* p. 317.

10. Frederick Law Olmsted, *Walks and Talks of an American Farmer in England* (New York: G. P. Putnam, 1852), p. 133.

11. Clarence Cook, *A Description of the New York Central Park* (New York: F. J. Huntington and Co., 1869), p. 81.

12. Ibid., p. 54.

13. For a good anthology of scholarly articles that discuss different cultural and social aspects of the "rural" cemetery movement in America, see David E. Stannard, ed., *Death in America* (Philadelphia: Univ. of Pennsylvania Press, 1974).

14. Quoted in Nicolai Cikovsky, Jr., ed., *Lectures on the Affinity of Painting with the Other Fine Arts* by Samuel F. B. Morse (Columbia, Mo.: Univ. of Missouri Press, 1983), p. 20.

15. For Jefferson's reliance on Thomas Whateley's *Observations of Modern Gardening,* see William H. Adams, ed., *The Eye of Thomas Jefferson* (Washington, D.C.: National Gallery of Art, 1976), p. 195; for Morse's citation of Whateley, see Cikovsky, Jr., ed., *Lectures on the Affinity of Painting,* pp. 80–82; Carleton Mabee, *The American Leonardo: A Life of Samuel F. B. Morse* (New York: Knopf, 1943); Oliver W. Larkin, *Samuel F. B. Morse and American Democratic Art* (Boston: Little, Brown, 1954); Paul J. Staiti, "Ideology and Politics in Samuel F. B. Morse's Agenda for a National Art," in *Samuel F. B. Morse: Educator and Champion of the Arts in America* (New York: National Academy of Design, 1982).

16. Cikovsky, Jr., ed., *Lectures on the Affinity of Painting,* pp. 58–59.

17. Edward Lind Morse, ed., *Samuel F. B. Morse: His Letters and Journals* II (Boston: Houghton Mifflin, 1914), pp. 269, 280–81.

18. Ibid., p. 281. Although Poughkeepsie officially was designated as a "village" in 1847, the term is misleading since it was clearly an important American urban settlement; see Harvey K. Flad, ". . . the hand of Art, when guided by Taste" and Matthew Vassar, "Springside"—revised version of paper delivered on May 16, 1987, at the symposium "Prophet with Honor: The Career of Andrew Jackson Downing (1815–1852)," at Dumbarton Oaks, Washington, D.C., p. 2. I am indebted to Dr. Flad for giving me a copy of his revised paper.

19. Quoted in Larkin, *Samuel F. B. Morse and American Democratic Art,* p. 191.

20. Quoted in Morse, ed., *Samuel F. B. Morse,* II, p. 471. For a comparison of Morse with Fulton, see Mabee, *The American Leonardo.*

21. For Clinton's contribution to the building of the Erie Canal, see Shaw, *Erie Water West;* Mabee, *The American Leonardo,* p. 100.

22. Shaw, *Erie Water West,* p. 135; Lossing, *The Hudson,* pp. 95, 111–12; Goodrich, *Government Promotion of American Canals and Railroads,* p. 56; Lossing, *The Hudson,* pp. 184–85.

23. For varying discussions on the changing American landscape, see Sanford, *The Quest for Paradise,* pp. 135–54; Laurence Goldstein, *Ruins and Empire: The Evolution of a Theme in Augustan and Romantic Literature* (Pittsburgh: Univ. of Pittsburgh Press, 1977), pp. 217–31; Noble, *The Eternal Adam and the New World Garden,* pp. 3–24; Matthew Baigell, *Thomas Cole* (New York: Watson-Guptil, 1981), pp. 19–26; Nash, *Wilderness and the American Mind,* p. 23; Patricia Anderson, *The Course of Empire: The Erie Canal and the New York Landscape, 1825–1875* (Rochester: Memorial Art Gallery of the Univ. of Rochester, 1984), pp. 13–17.

24. Anderson, *Course of Empire,* pp. 27–30

25. Shaw, *Erie Water West,* p. 87.

26. O'Brien, *American Sublime,* p. 131.

27. Benson J. Lossing, *Lives of Celebrated Americans: Comprising Biographies of Three Hundred and Forty Eminent Persons* (Hartford: Belknap, 1869), p. 258.

28. Quoted in Blake, *Water for the Cities,* p. 108.

29. Ibid., pp. 132–42.

30. Blake, *Water for the Cities,* p. 143.

31. Ibid., pp. 145–71.

32. Ibid., p. 169; Lossing, *The Hudson,* p. 412.

33. Lossing, *The Hudson*, pp. 309–10.

34. T[homas] Addison Richards, *Romance of American Landscape* (New York: Leavitt & Allen, 1855), pp. 23–24.

35. Condit, *The Port of New York*, p. 32.

36. Quoted in ibid., p. 33.

37. This is the thesis of the essays by Leo Marx and Kenneth W. Maddox in Susan Danly Walther, *The Railroad in the American Landscape: 1850–1950* (Wellesley, Mass.: Wellesley College Museum, 1981).

38. Mabee, *The American Leonardo*, pp. 356–57; Larkin, *Samuel F. B. Morse*, pp. 159–60; for an excellent contemporary description of Locust Grove, see Lossing, *The Hudson*, pp. 190–92.

39. Mabee, *The American Leonardo*, p. 357; Morse, *Samuel F. B. Morse*, II, pp. 496, 513. For a discussion of the movement to establish a "rural" cemetery in Poughkeepsie, see Flad, ". . . the hand of Art, when guided by Taste," pp. 2–6.

40. Harris, *The Artist in American Society*, pp. 200–8, 377–78; Stanley French, "The Cemetery as a Cultural Institution: The Establishment of Mount Auburn and the 'Rural Cemetery' Movement," *American Quarterly*, XXVI (March 1974), pp. 37–59.

41. In fact, as Flad has shown in his essay " . . . the hand of Art, when guided by Taste," the Poughkeepsie site designed as a summer estate by Andrew Jackson Downing with and for Matthew Vassar was originally designated and improved as a "rural" cemetery.

42. For a listing of famous people, notably artists, buried in Greenwood Cemetery, see *Now Reposing in Greenwood Cemetery* (New York: Museum of the Borough of Brooklyn, New York, 1986).

43. Allan Nevins, *The Evening Post* (New York: Boni and Livermore,1922), p. 356; James T. Callow, *Kindred Spirits: Knickerbocker Writers and American Artists, 1807–1855* (Chapel Hill, N.C.: Univ. of North Carolina Press, 1967), p. 64–69.

44. Parke Godwin, ed., *Prose Writings of William Cullen Bryant*, II: *Travels, Addresses, and Comments* (New York: Appleton & Co., 1884 [1964 ed.]), p. 279.

45. For an analysis of Bryant's changing social perspective, see Goldstein, *Ruins and Empire*, pp. 217–22.

46. Charles H. Brown, *William Cullen Bryant* (New York: Charles Scribner's Sons, 1971), pp. 291–93; Godwin, ed., *Prose Writings of William Cullen Bryant*, "The Utility of Trees," pp. 402–5; Lossing, *The Hudson*, p. 257.

47. William Cullen Bryant, "New York Evening Post," July 3, 1844, quoted in Nevins, *The Evening Post*, pp. 193–94. Of Bryant's six trips to Europe, the one taken in 1845 was probably the most influential in terms of studying European innovations in urban open-space planning and design: Godwin, ed., *Prose Writings of William Cullen Bryant*, p. 83; Brown, *William Cullen Bryant*, pp. 303–13.

48. William C. Bryant to Frances Bryant, October 13, 1847, Goddard-Roslyn Collection, Manuscript Division, New York Public Library.

49. Leonora Scott Cranch, ed., *The Life and Letters of Christopher Pearse Cranch* (Boston: Houghton Mifflin, 1917), p. 174; Frederick Law Olmsted, MS draft of "Introduction" to *Cottage Residences*, c. 1867, Frederick Law Olmsted Papers, Manuscript Division, Library of Congress. This revised edition of Downing's book was never published. The most perceptive biographical analysis of Downing to date is George William Curtis, ed., "Memoir of the Author," in *Rural Essays by A. J. Downing* (New York: Leavitt & Allen, 1857).

50. Attitudes toward immigrants varied widely. Morse, for example, forsook democratic principles to become a noted anti-Catholic propagandist in the 1830s, authoring influential pamphlets opposed to the integration of the foreign-born into American society: Larkin, *Samuel F. B. Morse*, pp. 121–25; William Cullen Bryant took the opposite point of view— "that of equal rights for all"—Brown, *William Cullen Bryant*, p. 234.

51. Andrew Jackson Downing, "Mr. Downing's Letters from England," *Horticulturist* (June 1, 1851), p. 286.

52. Albert Fein, "Centennial New York, 1876," in Milton M. Klein, ed., *New York: The Centennial Years, 1676–1976* (New York: Kennikat Press, 1976), pp. 97–98; Edward K. Spann, *The New Metropolis: New York City, 1840–1857* (New York: Columbia Univ. Press, 1981), Chap. XIV.

53. For a good description of the diverse cultural elements included in the mid-nineteenth-century consensus on nature, see Sydney Kurland, "The Aesthetic Quest of Thomas Cole & Edgar Allan Poe: Correspondences in Their Thought & Practice in Relation to Their Time" (Ph.D. dissertation, Ohio Univ., 1976), Chap. I. For Ruskin's influence in America, see Roger B. Stein, *John Ruskin and Aesthetic Thought in America, 1840–1900* (Cambridge, Mass.: Harvard University Press, 1967); as an example of *Putnam's* support for Durand's aesthetic ideas during Olmsted's period of ownership, see "The National Academy of Design," *Putnam's Monthly Magazine* V (May 1855), p. 506.

54. Asher B. Durand, "Letter II," *Crayon* I (January 17, 1855), p. 35; Durand, "Letter I," *Crayon* I (January 3, 1855), p. 2. Bryant's poem is quoted in, among other places, Flexner, *That Wilder Image*.

55. Calvert Vaux to the Editor, *New York Evening Post*, May 9, 1865.

56. Linda S. Ferber, " 'Determined Realists': The American Pre-Raphaelites and the Association for the Advancement of Truth in Art," in Linda S. Ferber and William H. Gerdts, *The New Path: Ruskin and the American Pre-Raphaelites* (Brooklyn Museum, New York, 1985).

57. Cook, *A Description of the New York Central Park*, pp. 108–9.

58. Lossing, *The Hudson*, pp. 397–98.

59. Ibid.; William Cullen Bryant, ed., *Picturesque America; or, the Land We Live In* VI (New York: Appleton & Co., 1872), pp. 555–57. For a fuller discussion of the park's relationship to public health, see Fein, *Frederick Law Olmsted and the American Environmental Tradition*, pp. 28–29; Fein, "History Section," in *The First Historic Landscape Report . . . Prospect Park, Brooklyn, New York*, pp. 9–12; James D. McCabe, Jr., *New York by Gaslight* (New York: Greenwich House, 1984, reprint of 1882 publication, *New York by Sunlight and Gaslight*, Hubbard Brothers).

60. Frederick Law Olmsted to Henry G. Stebbins, June 26, 1876, Olmsted Papers, Library of Congress. Bryant, ed., *Picturesque America* VI, p. 555.

61. Cook, *Central Park*, pp. 120–21.

62. Ibid., pp. 127–28. Downing also recommended rustic design for outdoor furniture and other objects. Downing, *A Treatise on the Theory and Practice of Landscape Gardening,* pp. 393–99.

63. Frederick Law Olmsted and Calvert Vaux, "Description of a Plan for the Improvement of the Central Park: 'Greensward' (1858–1868 reprint)," in Albert Fein, ed., *Landscape into Cityscape: Frederick Law Olmsted's Plans for a Greater New York City* (New York: Cornell Univ. Press, 1981), p. 66.

64. Flexner, *That Wilder Image,* p. xiii. For a full discussion of the historiography of the movement, see Kevin J. Avery, "A Historiography of the Hudson River School," in Howat et al., *American Paradise,* pp. 3–20; on the decline of interest in this school of artists, see Doreen Bolger Burke and Catherine Hoover Voorsanger, "The Hudson River School in Eclipse," in Howat et al., *American Paradise,* pp. 71–90.

65. Albert Fein, "Summary Report of the Study of the Profession of Landscape Architecture," *Landscape Architecture* (October 1972), pp. 34–47. The bibliography of books and articles included in Stevenson, *Park Maker,* pp. 457–61, reflects this increased interest. More than 50 percent of the items have been published since 1950; see also Fein, "The Olmsted Renaissance: A Search for National Purpose," *Landscape into Cityscape* (New York: Van Nostrand Reinhold, Co., 1981), Preface, pp. ix–xxiii.

66. Allan R. Talbot, *Power Along the Hudson; The Storm King Case and the Birth of Environmentalism* (New York: E. P. Dutton, 1972). For a description of efforts to restore the river, see Jack Hope and Robert Perron, *A River for the Living: The Hudson and Its People* (New York: Crown, 1975).

67. O'Brien, *American Sublime,* p. 29; Howat, *The Hudson River and Its Painters* (New York: American Legacy Press, 1972), pp. 7, 11; for an important updating of Howat's work, see his introduction and essay, "A Climate for Landscape Painters," in Howat et al., *American Paradise,* pp. xvii, 49–70.

68. Henry Hope Reed and Sophia Duckworth, *Central Park: A History and a Guide* (New York: Clarkson N. Potter, 1972), pp. 65–66, 113.

Chapter 2

1. See Bruce Robertson, "Venit, Vedit, Depinxit: The Military Artist in America," *Views and Visions: American Landscape before 1830* (Washington, D.C.: Corcoran Gallery of Art, 1986), pp. 83–93.

2. James Thacher, *Military Journal During the American Revolutionary War, from 1775 to 1783* (Hartford, Conn.: Silas Andrus & Son, 1854), p. 95.

3. Frances Trollope, *Domestic Manners of the Americans,* Donald Smalley, ed. (New York: Knopf, 1949 repr.), pp. 367–68.

4. Thomas Hamilton, *Men and Manners in America* (1833), quoted in Walter L. Creese, *The Crowning of the American Landscape* (Princeton: Princeton Univ. Press, 1985), p. 51.

5. Henry T. Tuckerman, *Artist-Life: or Sketches of American Painters* (New York: Appleton, 1847), p. 80.

6. (1825) Allen Art Museum, Oberlin College, Oberlin, Ohio.

7. Louis L. Noble, *The Life and Works of Thomas Cole,* Elliott S. Vesell, ed. (Cambridge, Mass.: Harvard Univ. Press, 1964), p. 148.

8. William Dunlap, *A History of the Rise and Progress of the Arts of Design in the United States,* II (New York: George P. Scott and Co., 1834), p. 360.

9. July 6, 1826. J. Bard McNulty, ed., *The Correspondence of Thomas Cole and Daniel Wadsworth* (Hartford: Connecticut Historical Society, 1983), p. 1.

10. (c. 1827) Museum of Fine Arts, Boston, and (1827) New Britain Museum of American Art, respectively.

11. (1826) Fort Ticonderoga Museum. The diminutive figures in the foreground represent participants in a tragic event from the American Revolution, popularized in James Fenimore Cooper's *The Last of the Mohicans.*

12. (1827–28) Museum of Fine Arts, Boston, and (1827) Wadsworth Atheneum, Hartford, respectively.

13. (1836) New-York Historical Society and (1839–40) Museum of Art, Munson-Williams-Proctor Institute, Utica, N.Y., respectively.

14. (1846) Brooklyn Museum. Quotation from Noble, *Life and Works,* p. 171.

15. "A Letter to Critics on the Art of Painting," *The Knickerbocker* (September 1840); "Sicillian Scenery and Antiquities," *The Knickerbocker* (February 1844 and March 1844).

16. Marshall Tymn, ed., "A Lecture on Art," *Thomas Cole: The Collected Essays and Prose Sketches* (St. Paul: John Colet Press, 1980), p. 108.

17. Marshall Tymn, ed., *Thomas Cole's Poetry* (York, Pa.: Liberty Cap Books, 1972), p. 67.

18. "Essay on American Scenery" was first published in the *American Monthly Magazine* (January 1836). Reprinted in Tymn, *Cole Essays,* pp. 3–17.

19. For a recent discussion, see Kenneth W. Maddox, "Thomas Cole and the Railroad: Gentle Maledictions," *Archives of American Art Journal* 26, 1 (1986), pp. 2–10.

20. Letter to Luman Reed, March 6, 1836 (Catskill). New York State Library, Albany.

21. (1837) Metropolitan Museum of Art, New York.

22. "Lecture on American Scenery: Delivered before The Catskill Lyceum, April 1, 1841" was first published in *Northern Light* (May 1841). Reprinted in Tymn, *Cole Essays,* pp. 197–212.

23. John Durand, *The Life and Times of A. B. Durand* (New York: Charles Scribner's Sons, 1894), p. 140. Facsimile reprinting (New York: Kennedy Graphics, Inc., Da Capo Press, 1970).

24. (c. 1885) Museum of Fine Arts, Boston.

25. Asher B. Durand, "Letters on Landscape Painting," *The Crayon* I (January–June 1855), p. 2.

26. Ibid., p. 34.

27. Ibid., II (July–December 1855), p. 274.

28. Letter to Thomas Cole, May 20, 1844. New York State Library, Albany.

29. *Hooker and Company Journeying through the Wilderness from Plymouth to Hartford in 1636* (1846), Wadsworth Atheneum, Hartford.

30. (1860) Cleveland Museum of Art.

31. David C. Huntington, *The Landscapes of Frederic Edwin Church* (New York: George Braziller, 1966), p. 83.

32. Ibid., p. 116.

33. Sanford R. Gifford, *Journal I* (entry for February 4, 1856). Archives of American Art, Washington, D.C. Typescript copy, p. 162.

34. (1849?) New-York Historical Society.

35. (1862) Metropolitan Museum of Art, New York.

36. (1866) Terra Museum of American Art, Chicago.

37. George W. Sheldon, "How a Landscape-Painter Paints," *Art Journal* III (1877), p. 284.

38. Jasper F. Cropsey, "Essay on Natural Art," written for The New York Art Reunion, August 24, 1845.

39. (1851) Cleveland Museum of Art.

40. (1855) Minneapolis Institute of Arts.

41. Thomas Cole, *The Catskill Mountain House* (1844), Brooklyn Museum.

42. Jasper F. Cropsey, "Up Among the Clouds," *The Crayon* II (August 1855), p. 79.

43. (1860) National Gallery of Art. The scene embraces a panoramic view of the Hudson between Newburgh and West Point.

44. *The Crayon* X (September 1859).

45. (1859) Museum of Fine Arts, Boston.

46. (1867) St. Johnsbury Athenaeum, St. Johnsbury, Vt.

47. *The Last of the Buffalo* (1888), Corcoran Gallery of Art, Washington, D.C. Even though the gallery's founder, William Wilson Corcoran, was one of Bierstadt's best clients, he did not purchase the painting; it was donated to the gallery by the artist's widow.

48. (c. 1855) National Gallery of Art.

49. "A Painter on Painting," *Harper's New Monthly Magazine* LVI (February 1878), p. 461.

50. George Inness, Jr., *Life, Art, and Letters of George Inness* (New York: The Century Co., 1917), p. 148.

51. Ibid., p. 157.

52. Letter, March 23, 1884. Quoted in N. Spassky, *American Paintings in the Metropolitan Museum of Art* II (New York: Metropolitan Museum of Art and Princeton Univ. Press, 1985), p. 264.

53. Letter, January 4, 1838. Noble, *Life and Times*, p. 185.

54. Roland Van Zandt, *The Catskill Mountain House* (Cornwallville, N.Y.: Hope Farm Press, 1982), p. 292.

Chapter 3

1. Candace Wheeler, "The Painters of Yesterday," 1900, memoirs of her friendships with artists, from a typescript in the Museum of Fine Arts, Boston, Department of Prints, Drawings and Photographs, pp. 11–12.

2. Asher B. Durand, "Letters on Landscape Painting, I," *The Crayon* V (1855), p. 2.

3. Thus the stereoscope—portable, exact, and rendering a sense of depth—was certainly related to the panorama, or at least addressed some of the same interests. See Lee Parry, "Landscape Theatre in America," *Art in America* 59 (November 1971), pp. 52–61, who discusses the relationship of panoramas to landscape painters, especially Thomas Cole; Barbara Novak, "Grand Opera and the Small Still Voice," in *Nature and Culture: American Landscape and Painting, 1825–1875* (New York: Oxford Univ. Press, 1980), Chap. II; and Henry M. Sayre, "Surveying the Vast Profound; the Panoramic Landscape in American Consciousness," *Massachusetts Review* 24 (Winter 1983), pp. 723–42. Panoramas and topographical representation in mid-century drawings are wonderfully analyzed by Linda S. Ferber in *American Light: The Luminist Movement, 1850–1875, Paintings, Drawings, Photographs* (Washington, D.C.: National Gallery of Art, 1980), pp. 255ff. The related use of optical devices by many mid-century landscape artists is admirably discussed by Lisa Fellows Andrus in her *Measure and Design in American Painting, 1760–1860* (New York, 1977), Chap. 6.

4. Preface to *Harvey's Scenes in the Primeval Forests of America. . . .* (London, 1841), p. 4. Many thanks to Stephen Eden, curator at Montclair Art Museum, for sharing his insights and information on George Harvey.

5. See Koke, *American Landscape and Genre Paintings in the New-York Historical Society* 2, p. 100; Donald A. Shelley, "George Harvey and His Atmospheric Landscapes of North America," *New-York Historical Society Quarterly* V (April 1948), pp. 104–13. Albert Bierstadt is known to have displayed the Harvey lantern slides as a young man in New Bedford. See Gordon Hendricks, *Albert Bierstadt*, p. 17.

6. See John Henry Hill, *John William Hill: An Artist's Memorial.* (New York: 1888) I am most indebted to Martica Sawin for her knowledge of the Hills; see her catalogue, *John William Hill, John Henry Hill* (New York: Washburn Gallery, 1973). I would also like to thank John Scott and Lynne Beaman for their assistance. See also Roger B. Stein, *John Ruskin and Aesthetic Thought in America, 1840–1900* (Cambridge, Mass.: Harvard Univ. Press, 1967), p. 41.

7. For a comparison of a work by Hill with a photograph by O'Sullivan of the same site (Shoshone Falls), see Weston J. Naef and James N. Wood, with an essay by Therese Thau Heyman, *Era of Exploration: The Rise of Landscape Photography in the American West, 1860–1885* (New York: Albright-Knox Art Gallery and Metropolitan Museum of Art, 1975), p. 64. Besides the mentioned sources, much of this information comes from John Scott, "The Hill Family of Clarksville," *South of the Mountains, The Historical Society of Rockland County* 19 (January–March 1975), pp. 5–18.

8. Harry P. Havell, "Robert Havell's View of the Hudson

from Tarrytown Heights," *New-York Historical Society Quarterly* V (July 1947), pp. 160–62. Also typescript of a lecture by Robert B. Pattison to the Ossining Historical Society, "Robert Havell, Jr. and Havell Street."

9. Benson H. Lossing, *The Hudson from the Wilderness to the Sea. Illustrated by Three Hundred and Six Engravings on Wood from Drawings by the Author* (London: Virtue, 1866), p. 226.

10. Theodore Sizer, ed., *The Recollections of John Ferguson Weir, Director of the Yale School of the Fine Arts, 1869–1913* (New Haven: Yale Univ. Press, 1957), pp. 37–38, 46.

11. Dr. Betsy Fahlman has kindly shared with me the following information on Weir (as well as other insights). A contemporary critic of 1865 quoted in Irene Weir, *Robert W. Weir, Artist* (New York: House of Field–Doubleday, 1947), p. 59. Also see *The Knickerbocker* (January 1851), pp. 41–42; and "An Artist at Home," *The Evening Post*, N.Y., October 7, 1877. I would like to thank Michael Moss, curator at West Point, and Marie Capps of the Special Collections for assisting me with Weir material.

12. Noble, *Life and Works*, pp. 184–85, 308–11; Barbara Novak, *American Painting of the Nineteenth Century: Realism, Idealism, and the American Experience* (New York: Praeger, 1971), pp. 77–79, esp. p. 79; Lisa Fellows Andrus, "Design and Measurement in American Art," in *American Light*; and Lee Parry, "Gothic Elegies for an American Audience: Thomas Cole's Repackaging of Imported Ideas," *American Art Journal* (November 1976), p. 46.

13. Letter of F. E. Church to Thomas Cole from Hartford, May 20, 1844, in the Thomas Cole Papers, New York State Library, Albany (DJ 10635, Box 3, folder 5).

14. This essay was presented to the Art Union. A typescript is in the Print Room of the Museum of Fine Arts, Boston.

15. *American Art Journal* XVI (Summer 1984), p. 81.

16. Two of these are in the New-York Historical Society (nos. 1947.420 and 1947.421).

17. See Catherine Campbell, "Benjamin Bellows Grant Stone: A Forgotten American Artist," *New-York Historical Society Quarterly* V (January 1978), pp. 23ff. Campbell also describes his work for Prang and other reproductive companies. See the Benjamin Stone Papers, Bronck House, Coxsakie, N.Y.

18. Gifford, as quoted in Campbell, p. 40.

19. R. Lionel De Lisser, *Picturesque Catskills: Greene County* (Northampton, Mass.: Picturesque Publishing, 1894).

20. From annotations to sketches in the Bronck House, Coxsakie, N.Y. Clarence Cook, the great defender of the American Pre-Raphaelites, wrote a touching memorial describing the way A. J. Downing's grounds looked shortly after his death. See *The Horticulturalist* 8 (January 1853), pp. 21–27.

21. Quote from "The Artist's Fund Society, Fourth Annual Exhibition," *The New Path* I (December 1863), p. 98.

22. Linda S. Ferber, " 'Determined Realists': The American Pre-Raphaelites and the Association for the Advancement of Truth in Art," in *The New Path*, 1985.

23. See *The New Path*, pp. 196, 201.

24. The letter dated "Catskill, N.Y., Feb. 12th 1866" is in the New York State Museum, Albany. The article was titled "Materials for Landscape Art in America" (see pp. 671–72).

He also made both a drawing and a painting of this subject in 1868, now at the Princeton University Art Museum.

25. Information on Robert Fulton Ludlow is almost entirely drawn from the photographic negatives and records at the Columbia County Historical Society, Kinderhook, N.Y.

26. From a letter first quoted by Samuel Ireneaus Prime in *The Life of Samuel F. B. Morse* (New York: Appleton and Co., 1875), 401.

27. Morse himself practiced daguerreotypy shortly after his return to America, while awaiting the patenting of his telegraph, and worked particularly on portraiture. Benson J. Lossing also describes Morse's photographic experiments and brief career as a photographer in his essay, "Professor Morse and the Telegraph," *Scribner's Monthly* 5 (March 1875), pp. 584–85.

28. See Prime, *Life of Morse*, p. 400.

29. Rossiter's collection of photographs is described in the last auction of his works and effects, *Catalogue of Valuable Antique Furniture, Paintings, Engravings and Books, Articles of Vertu and Curiosities, To be Sold at Auction Feb. 5–8*, Clinton Hall, N.Y., 1873.

30. See Lossing, p. 246. The preceding page has Lossing's own view of the scene. In her M.A. thesis on the artist, Ilene Susan Fort maintains that Rossiter probably used photographs in his portraiture, which may account for the rather detached nature of some of the group portraits. See *High Art and the American Experience: The Career of Thomas Pritchard Rossiter*, Queens College, M.A. thesis, 1975.

31. Worthington Whittredge in *Gifford Memorial Meeting of the Century* (New York: Century Association, 1880), p. 33. Gifford's brother, Charles, was a landscape architect.

32. Ila Weiss has noted evidence of interest in photography in *Sanford Robinson Gifford (1823–1880)* (New York: Garland, 1977), p. 128. There is also much circumstantial evidence linking Gifford to photography. Many of his European pictures, for instance, are painted of well-known views known to have been photographed at the time. See the Gifford Papers at the Albany Institute of History and Art and the Archives of American Art, Roll 672, which contains miscellaneous photographs collected by Gifford.

33. For information on Palmer, see the extensive biography by J. Carson Webster, *Erastus D. Palmer* (Newark, Del.: Univ. of Delaware Press, 1983). The relationship of Palmer and Church is documented in their correspondence at the Albany Institute of History and Art and at Olana.

34. For information on Palmer, in addition to the archival material at the Albany Institute of History and Art, see Maybelle Mann, *Walter Launt Palmer, Poetic Reality*, with catalogue raisonné by Alvin Lloyd Mann (Exton, Pa.: Schiffer, 1984).

35. Letter from Church to E. D. Palmer at the Albany Institute of History and Art. See Peter L. Goss, *An Investigation of Olana, The Home of Frederic Edwin Church*, Ohio University, Ph.D. dissertation, 1973, p. 8 and passim.

36. For an examination of Church's interest in photography, see Elizabeth Lindquist-Cock, "Frederic Church's Stereographic Vision," *Art in America* 62 (1973), pp. 70–75. David C. Huntington, *The Landscapes of Frederic Edwin Church:*

Vision of an American Era (New York: George Braziller, 1966) also considers photography in Church's work. For Church's own photographs of his site, gradually growing wilder the farther from the house they were made (in accordance with Downing's ideas), see Goss, pp. 107ff.

37. For information on the Vaux residence and painting, I am indebted to Herbert Shultz and Lowell Thing. For information on the Bierstadt mansion, as well as the artist's interest in photography, see Hendricks, *Bierstadt*, and Jennie Prince Black, *I Remember* (New York: 1938) I also thank Mrs. Orville de Forest Edwards, Bierstadt's grandniece. See Elizabeth Lindquist-Cock, "Stereoscopic Photography and the Western Paintings of Albert Bierstadt," *Art Quarterly* 33 (1970), pp. 361–78.

38. The clearest indication of Henry's extensive interest in photography is the large collection of photographs in the New York State Museum, which come directly from him. For a discussion of Henry's indebtedness to photography and examples of paintings made almost directly after photographs, see Elizabeth McCausland, *The Life and Work of Edward Lamson Henry, N.A., 1841–1919* (New York: Kennedy Graphics and Da Capo Press, 1970), pp. 270–71. See also Barbara Buff, "Cragsmoor, an Early American Art Colony," *Magazine Antiques* (November 1978), pp. 1055–67.

39. Besides Dellenbaugh's own book, *A Canyon Voyage, The Narrative of the Second Powell Expedition . . . in the Years 1871 and 1872* (New York and London, 1908), see also Robert Taft, *Photography and the American Scene, A Social History, 1839–1889* (New York: Dover, 1964), pp. 289ff and 494.

40. Although there are no photographs by Dellenbaugh in his papers, see his article "A New Valley of Wonders," in *Scribner's Magazine* XXXV (January 1904), pp. 1–18, illus-trated with photographs by the author. Another Cragsmoor resident, George Inness, Jr., participated in the documentation of the spectacular views of the Far West. See Thomas Moran, "American Art and American Scenery," *Grand Canyon of Arizona*, published by the Passenger Department of the Santa Fe Railroad, 1902, pp. 85–87, about his trip there with George Inness, Jr.

41. As stated in *The Cragsmoor Artists' Vision of Nature, An Exhibition of Paintings by Cragsmoor Artists*, catalogue for exhibition at Cragsmoor and State Univ. of New York, New Paltz, 1977. Essays by Maybelle Mann and Kaycee Benton.

42. Information on Candace Wheeler and Onteora can be found in her autobiography, *Yesterdays in a Busy Life* (New York: Harper and Bros., 1917), and G. Frederick Hawkins, *A Short History of the Onteora Club*, excerpts from a talk at the Mountain Top Historical Society, August 28, 1975. See also Wilson H. Faude, "Associated Artists and the American Renaissance in the Decorative Arts," *Winterthur Portfolio* 10 (1975), pp. 101–30.

43. For information on Inness, besides the usual sources, I have consulted with Nicolai Cikovsky, Jr. See his contribution to *George Inness* (Los Angeles County Museum of Art, 1985–86), esp. p. 12 and a discussion of Inness's lack of specificity of place: "When asked where a picture was painted, he replied, 'Nowhere in particular; do you suppose I illustrate guide-books? That's a picture.'"

44. For information on the Pakatakan colony, with particular reference to the Murphys, see the Emerson Crosby Kelly Papers in the Archives of American Art, which include Dr. Kelly's typescript biography of Murphy, and Murphy diaries, letters, books, drawings, and material of Mrs. Murphy, including many photographs.

Chapter 4

In addition to those persons whose help is acknowledged in individual footnotes, I wish to recognize Sandra S. Phillips, who generously shared with me her extensive research on this topic. I also acknowledge the assistance of a grant from the Greene County Council on the Arts.

1. Lizzie W. Champney, "The Summer Haunts of American Artists," *Century Magazine* 30 (October 1885), pp. 845–46.

2. Artists who built houses and studios in the Hudson Valley and Catskills did not create new styles (with the possible exception of Charles Herbert Moore's revival of the old Dutch farmhouse) but rather chose among the styles already defined by architects. Mark Girouard, *Sweetness and Light: The "Queen Anne" Movement* (Oxford: Oxford Univ. Press, 1977), p. 97, has found the same to be true of studio-houses in late nineteenth-century England.

3. M. Phipps-Jackson, "Cairo in London: Carl Haag's Studio," *Art Journal* 35 (1883), p. 71, concluded that "in many of the leading studios . . . one finds the mind of the master curiously apparent, for . . . a painter's . . . artistic tastes and sympathies are to be discovered in the abode he has chosen."

4. Jules David Prown, *John Singleton Copley*, 2 vols. (Cambridge, Mass.: Harvard Univ. Press, 1966), I, p. 66; Girouard, *Sweetness and Light,* pp. 99, 103.

5. Roland Van Zandt, *The Catskill Mountain House* (New Brunswick: Rutgers Univ. Press, 1966), p. 175; John Durand, *The Life and Times of A. B. Durand* (New York: Scribner's, 1894; repr. New York: Da Capo Press, 1970), pp. 185–86.

6. Van Zandt, *Catskill Mountain House,* p. 366.

7. Jervis McEntee to Mrs. Monnell, May 30, 1886, Archives of American Art.

8. Drawing by Jameson in author's collection. T. Addison Richards, "The Catskills," *Harper's New Monthly Magazine* 9 (July 1854), pp. 156–57, describes such a "bough house."

9. Asher B. Durand, "Letters on Landscape Painting. Letter 1," *The Crayon* 1 (January 3, 1855), p. 2; Richards, "Catskills," p. 153.

10. Richards, "Catskills," p. 151; Durand, *Life and Times,* p. 184.

11. Horace J. Rollin, *Studio, Field and Gallery: A Manual of Painting for the Student and Amateur* (New York: Appleton, 1878), pp. 92–93. The studios of landscape painters were

usually smaller and simpler than those of figure painters, who, for example, required a special entrance for (not quite respectable) models. See Maurice B. Adams, *Artists' Homes* (London: B. T. Batsford, 1883), p. 10.

12. Harry B. Harvey, "Village Historian Relates Hastings Past," *Hastings News*, July 29, 1959; Kenneth W. Maddox, "The Hastings Waterfront," *Hastings Historical Society Newsletter* (July 1983), p. 2; *Harvey's Royal Gallery of Illustration . . . The Scenery, Resources, and Progress of North America* (London, n.d.), pp. 4, 17. Harvey sold his house in 1847; it was demolished in the 1960s (Mary L. Allison to Sandra S. Phillips, July 10, 1985).

13. Noble, *Life and Works*, p. 46.

14. Raymond Beecher, "Cedar Grove—The Thomas Cole Residence," *The Crayon* 12 (Spring 1980), pp. 1, 5–7.

15. Jasper Cropsey in 1850 called the house "old fashion, rather a mixture of the old fashioned dutch and English." Cropsey to his wife, July 7, 1850, *American Art Journal* 16 (Summer 1984), p. 81.

16. Thomas Cole, "Essay on American Scenery" (1835), in John W. McCoubrey, *American Art 1700–1960 Sources and Documents* (Englewood Cliffs, N.J.: Prentice-Hall, 1965), p. 102. Cole could not fathom how his friend Durand could prefer Newburgh: "I fear there is little rich forest scenery near, and few fine isolated trees; and, as for mountains, where are the Catskills?" Cole to Durand, August 7, 1838, in Noble, *Life and Works*, p. 199. Durand went against Cole's advice and in 1849 purchased a property near Newburgh with a view across the Hudson. Durand, *Life and Times*, p. 184.

17. Cropsey to his wife, July 7, 1850, *American Art Journal* 16 (Summer 1984), pp. 81–82.

18. Henry T. Tuckerman, *Book of the Artists: American Artist Life* (1867; repr. New York: James F. Carr, 1966), p. 223.

19. Allen to Cole, February 2 (?), 1837, Thomas Cole Papers, New York State Library, Albany, reel 2; Ellwood C. Parry III, "Thomas Cole's 'The Hunter's Return'," *American Art Journal* 17 (Summer 1985), 9; Cole to William A. Adams, April 8, 1841, in Noble, *Life and Works*, p. 219.

20. Parry, "Hunter's Return," pp. 8–9; Donelson Hoopes to author, September 27, 1986, suggests that the drawings may be for "an entirely new residence."

21. Andrew Jackson Downing, *A Treatise on the Theory and Practice of Landscape Gardening* (New York: Riker, Thorne, 1854), pp. 379–80.

22. Henry-Russell Hitchcock, *Architecture: Nineteenth and Twentieth Centuries* (Baltimore: Penguin, 1971), pp. 27, 64; J. B. Papworth, *Rural Residences* (London, 1818), quoted by Henry-Russell Hitchcock, *Early Victorian Architecture in Britain*, 2 vols. (New Haven: Yale Univ. Press, 1954), I, p. 30.

23. Downing, *Treatise*, pp. 391, 412; Andrew Jackson Downing, *The Architecture of Country Houses* (New York: Appleton, 1851), pp. 290–91.

24. Wayne Craven, "Thomas Cole and Italy," *Magazine Antiques* 114 (November 1978), pp. 1016–27, plates I, V, VII–X.

25. Thomas Cole, "Letter to the Publick on the Subject of Architecture," Cole Papers, New York State Library, reel 1.

26. The building survives, but few traces of the studio remain.

27. Cole to Durand, December 18, 1839, in Noble, *Life and Works*, p. 206.

28. Noble, *Life and Works*, p. 279; Cropsey to his wife, July 7, 1850, *American Art Journal* 16 (Summer 1984), p. 81; Cole, "Essay on American Scenery," p. 106. Cropsey described the studio as "large and comodious [*sic*] with a neat little porch and a wide open hall before entering the painting department"—the high-ceilinged room that occupied most of the building.

29. Drawings and correspondence by Morse and Davis at the Young-Morse Historic Site, Poughkeepsie, and the Metropolitan Museum of Art; *Samuel F. B. Morse* (New York: New York Univ., 1982), p. 80.

30. Edward Lind Morse, ed., *Samuel F. B. Morse: His Letters and Journals*, 2 vols. (Boston: Houghton Mifflin, 1914), II, pp. 280–81.

31. E. L. Morse, ed., *Morse*, I, p. 329; *Morse* (New York: New York Univ., 1982), pp. 62, 64.

32. Thomas P. Rossiter to Robert W. Gibbes, November 1844, in Robert W. Gibbes, *A Memoir of James DeVeaux* (Columbia, S.C.: I. C. Morgan, 1846), p. 241; Margaret Broaddus, "Thomas P. Rossiter," *American Art and Antiques* 2 (May–June 1979), p. 112; Paul R. Baker, *Richard Morris Hunt* (Cambridge, Mass.: MIT Press, 1980), pp. 80–82; Tuckerman, *Book of the Artists*, p. 435; Benson J. Lossing, *The Hudson from the Wilderness to the Sea* (New York: Virtue and Yorston, 1866), p. 246.

33. Carl Oechsner, *Ossining, N.Y.* (Croton-on-Hudson: North River Press, 1975), p. 55.

34. Nicolai Cikovsky, Jr., *Sanford Robinson Gifford* (Austin: Univ. of Texas Art Museum, 1970), pp. 8, 13; Ila Weiss to Sandra S. Phillips, May 15, 1986. The Gifford house no longer stands.

35. Worthington Whittredge, *Autobiography* (New York: Arno, 1969), p. 60.

36. T. B. Aldrich, "Among the Studios," *Our Young Folks 2* (October 1866), p. 625; Calvert Vaux, *Villas and Cottages* (New York: Harper, 1857), pp. 153–56. The engraved view of the studio bears Vaux's monogram. The date (c. 1853) is suggested by a diary entry of October 28, 1880, which refers to a stove being put up in the studio "at least twenty-seven years ago." Jervis McEntee diary (New-York Historical Society), available on microfilm through the Archives of American Art.

37. McEntee diary, July 29, 1873.

38. McEntee diary, November 1, 1883; the view of the cottage as it was to be completed bears the initials of Frederick C. Withers.

39. Vaux, *Villas and Cottages*, pp. 153–55. Aldrich, "Among the Studios," p. 623, commented that McEntee's Rondout studio was "most romantically situated."

40. G. W. Sheldon, *American Painters* (New York: Appleton, 1879), pp. 52–53. No trace of McEntee's studio-house has been found in Rondout.

41. Frank Jewett Mather, Jr., *Charles Herbert Moore* (Princeton: Princeton Univ. Press, 1957); Ferber and Gerdts, *The New Path*; C. H. Moore to C. E. Norton, February 12, 1866, New York State Museum–History Collections, Albany.

42. The Moore house first appears in the tax book of the town of Catskill in 1869 as owned by his wife, on twenty-three acres, and valued at four thousand dollars. Craig Mawhirt provided this and other information about the Moore property.

43. "House-Building in America," *Putnam's Monthly* 10 (July 1857), p. 111 (Ellen Kramer, "The Domestic Architecture of Detlef Lienau," Ph.D. dissertation, New York Univ., 1957, 232, attributed the article to Wight); W., "What Has Been Done," *New Path* 1 (September 1863), p. 54. Wight made drawings for Gothic Revival furniture for Moore: Sarah Bradford Landau, *P. B. Wight: Architect, Contractor, and Critic* (Chicago: Art Institute of Chicago, 1981), pp. 19, 96, 97. There is no evidence that Wight designed the Lodge: Sarah Bradford Landau to author, October 9, 1984. Frank Jewett Mather, who knew Moore's daughter, believed Moore designed the cottage himself (Mather, *Moore*, p. 23). The Moore house exists, though it became an appendage of a larger house designed by K. C. Budd and completed in 1902 for the Howland family. Documents regarding this house are in the Greene County Historical Society. In 1984 extensive alterations were made to the Moore portion. The house is inaccurately located on the map published in John Zukowsky and Robbe Pierce Stimson, *Hudson River Villas* (New York: Rizzoli, 1985).

44. Martha J. Lamb, *The Homes of America* (New York: Appleton, 1879), p. 151, notes that De Tocqueville, when visiting Irving, was much impressed with the view from what became Malkasten's site.

45. Tuckerman, *Book of the Artists*, pp. 396–97. Tuckerman also pointed out the ease of reaching New York City from Irvington and the proximity of cultivated neighbors.

46. Lamb, *Homes*, p. 151.

47. Hendricks, *Bierstadt*, pp. 167–72, 274–75; Jennie Prince Black, *I Remember* (New York: privately printed, 1938), p. 26; Lamb, *Homes*, p. 151. Little is known of the layout of the grounds, but Bierstadt said they were "especially arranged with a view to painting animals under the best possible conditions of light and shade and background." Hendricks, *Bierstadt*, p. 275.

48. Zukowsky and Stimson, *Hudson River Villas*, p. 87; Hendricks, *Bierstadt*, p. 275.

49. Hendricks, *Bierstadt*, pp. 167–72, 273–76.

50. Downing, *Treatise*, p. 378; William S. Talbot, *Jasper F. Cropsey 1823–1900* (New York: Garland, 1977), pp. 21, 25.

51. William Henry Forman, "Jasper Francis Cropsey, N.A.," *The Manhattan An Illustrated Monthly* (April 1884), p. 379; Talbot, *Cropsey*, p. 223.

52. Forman, "Cropsey," p. 379.

53. Talbot, *Cropsey*, p. 223; F. W., "Art-Home in the Hills," *Home Journal* (October 18, 1871). I thank Florence Levins of the Cropsey-Newington Foundation for providing a copy of this article.

54. F. W., "Art-Home"; Forman, "Cropsey" pp. 379–80.

55. Forman, "Cropsey," p. 380; F. W., "Art-Home."

56. F. W., "Art-Home."

57. F. W., "Art-Home"; Talbot, *Cropsey*, p. 230; William Nathaniel Banks, "Ever Rest, Jasper Francis Cropsey's House," *Magazine Antiques* 130 (November 1986), p. 1003.

58. National Register of Historic Places, Inventory-Nomination Form, Cropsey-Newington Foundation; Julia Markus, "Jasper Cropsey's Resonant Rooms Come to Life Again," *Smithsonian* 10 (January 1980), p. 107. Cropsey's drawings for the Hastings studio are still in the house.

59. Talbot, *Cropsey*, pp. 231–32. The property has been preserved as an historic site through the Cropsey-Newington Foundation.

60. McEntee diary, July 22, 1872. The best descriptions and analyses of Olana are David C. Huntington, *The Landscapes of Frederic Edwin Church* (New York: George Braziller, 1966), pp. 114–25; Clive Aslet, "Olana, New York State," *Country Life* 174 (September 22 and 29, 1983), pp. 761–65, 839–42; and James Ryan, "The Master Plan for Olana State Historic Site," M.A. thesis, State Univ. of New York, College at Oneonta, 1984. I also thank James Ryan for his suggestions after reading the portion of this essay concerning Olana. See also Peter L. Goss, "An Investigation of Olana," Ph.D. dissertation, Ohio Univ., 1973.

61. Huntington, *Church*, pp. 117–18; Susan R. Stein, ed., *The Architecture of Richard Morris Hunt* (Chicago: Univ. of Chicago Press, 1986), p. 113.

62. Aslet, "Olana," p. 763; F. E. Church to A. C. Goodman, July 21, 1871, quoted by Aslet, "Olana," p. 764. Some of the drawings for Olana dated May–June 1870 are in the hand of Withers according to Francis R. Kowsky, *The Architecture of Frederick Clarke Withers* (Middletown, Conn.: Wesleyan Univ. Press, 1980), p. 180.

63. Huntington, *Church*, p. 114; Aslet, "Olana," p. 765; Lamb, *Homes*, p. 176; F. E. Church to J. F. Weir, February 17, 1871, quoted by Ryan, "Master Plan," p. 32.

64. Vaux, *Villas and Cottages*, 2nd ed., pp. 81, 291; Kowsky, *Withers*, p. 96.

65. Christian Intelligencer, September 10, 1884, p. 2, quoted by Ryan, "Master Plan," p. 36; Roger B. Stein, "Artifact as Ideology: The Aesthetic Movement in Its American Cultural Context," in *In Pursuit of Beauty* (New York: Metropolitan Museum of Art, 1986), pp. 24–27.

66. McEntee diary, July 18, 1888. McEntee noted that Church "has torn down his old studio." This small studio appears indistinctly in an 1880s photo in the Olana archives. See Thomas O'Sullivan, "Studios of Victorian Artists," *The Crayon* 12 (Summer 1980), p. 6.

67. Thomas O'Sullivan, "The Studio Wing of Olana," *The Crayon* 11 (Fall 1979), pp. 1, 4–7. It has also been observed that the studio "tower's woodwork was painted in a combination of brick red and yellow-brown earth colors strikingly similar to color in the Mexican landscapes and cityscapes which Church painted during the 1880s." *DHP News*, No. 5 (Winter 1980).

68. Aslet, "Olana," pp. 840–42; Huntington, *Church*, p. 116.

69. Stein, "Artifact," p. 24.

70. "Landmark Gone," *Catskill Recorder*, December 9, 1921 (Justine Hommel of the Haines Falls Free Library provided this reference); Clara Erskine Clement and Laurence Hutton, *Artists of the Nineteenth Century* (Boston: Houghton Mifflin, 1894), p. 325. After Hall's death in 1913, a pupil, Jennie Brownscombe, took over the studio until its destruction by fire in 1921.

71. *Dictionary of American Biography*; Maitland Armstrong, *Day before Yesterday* (New York: Scribner's, 1920), pp. 329–31; Marion Edey, *Early in the Morning* (New York: Harper, 1954), p. 10; Gail E. Husch, "David Maitland Armstrong," *Magazine Antiques* 126 (November 1984), p. 1180; Hamilton Fish Armstrong, *Those Days* (New York: Harper and Row, 1963), pp. 138–39. The Armstrong house was demolished in 1977.

72. Helen Ver Nooy Gearn, "George Inness," *Historical Society of Newburgh Bay and the Highlands Publication 41* (1956), p. 7; Champney, "Summer Haunts," p. 846.

73. The Rondout and Oswego Railroad penetrated this part of the Catskills in 1870.

74. A. W. Dimock, a New York financier and friend of Ward, took credit for discovering the Peekamoose site in the 1870s: A. W. Dimock, *Wall Street and the Wilds* (New York: Outing, 1915), p. 385. See also Lewis I. Sharp, *John Quincy Adams Ward* (Newark, Del.: Univ. of Delaware Press, 1985), pp. 18, 220.

75. Sharp, *Ward*, fig. 51, illustrates a c. 1890 photo of the Peekamoose Fishing Club with a bust of A. W. Dimock, carved by Ward from a tree trunk, standing outside the log cabin.

76. McEntee diary, July 21, 1884, describes his encounter with Mrs. Wentworth, who was trying to paint a view of Peekamoose with the cabin.

77. De Lisser, *Picturesque Ulster,* pp. 146–48; Alf Evers, *The Catskills* (Garden City, N.Y.: Doubleday, 1972), pp. 594–95.

78. De Lisser, *Picturesque Ulster,* p. 148; *The Collector* 7 (September 15, 1896), p. 291 (reference provided by Lewis I. Sharp).

79. De Lisser, *Picturesque Ulster,* p. 148. The fireplace in the enlarged cottage is dated 1898; however, Sharp, *Ward,* p. 66, gives c. 1885 as the date for a photo of the transformed cottage.

80. Sharp to author, July 31, 1984; Sharp, *Ward,* p. 63.

81. Although no documentation has come to light, Richard Morris Hunt may have designed the Nordic additions: he had designed three earlier houses and/or studios for Ward and had traveled to Norway in 1867 and occasionally referred to its picturesque wooden buildings in his subsequent work. Sharp, *Ward,* pp. 23–24; Paul R. Baker, *Richard Morris Hunt* (Cambridge, Mass.: MIT Press, 1980), pp. 159, 271, and passim.

82. Barbara Buff, "Cragsmoor, An Early American Art Colony," *Magazine Antiques* 114 (November 1978), p. 1056; Barbara Ball Buff, "Mr. Henry of Cragsmoor," *Archives of American Art Journal* 21 (1981), pp. 2–7; Elizabeth McCausland, *The Life and Work of Edward Lamson Henry, N.A., 1841–1919* (Albany: Univ. of the State of New York, 1945), pp. 38–39.

83. For studios influenced by a taste for the colonial, see Celia Betsky, "Inside the Past: The Interior and the Colonial Revival in American Art and Literature, 1860–1914," in Alan Axelrod, ed., *The Colonial Revival in America* (New York: Norton, 1985), pp. 255–58.

84. McCausland, *Henry,* pp. 38–50; Champney, "Summer Haunts," p. 847. Vaux, *Villas and Cottages,* p. 71, proposed that covering a building with shingles cut in ornamental patterns was sanctioned by the precedent of Dutch settlers: Henry's house had such shingles.

85. *Dictionary of American Biography,* supplement 1; Frederick S. Dellenbaugh, *The North Americans of Yesterday* (New York: Putnam's, 1906), p. 195.

86. For Candace Wheeler's life and work, see her autobiography, *Yesterdays in a Busy Life* (New York: Harper, 1918), and Catherine Hoover Voorsanger in *In Pursuit of Beauty*, pp. 481–83.

87. Wheeler, *Yesterdays,* pp. 268–73; Gerald M. Best, *The Ulster and Delaware . . . Railroad through the Catskills* (San Marino, Calif.: Golden West, 1972), pp. 39–40. The early history of Onteora is also discussed by Evers, *Catskills,* pp. 538–43. Mrs. Wheeler recalled leaving the train at Phoenicia, though by 1883 a line extended through Stony Clove.

88. Wheeler, *Yesterdays,* pp. 273, 277–79, 282; Candace Wheeler, *Principles of Home Decoration* (New York: Doubleday, Page, 1903), pp. 58–59, 120, 124; Candace Wheeler, *The Annals of Onteora 1887–1914* (New York: privately printed, n.d.), p. 27. See James D. Kornwolf, "American Architecture and the Aesthetic Movement," in *In Pursuit of Beauty,* p. 368, for the movement's appreciation of vernacular design.

89. Wheeler, *Yesterdays,* pp. 279–80, 294; Wheeler, *Home Decoration,* p. 152; Candace Wheeler, *Content in a Garden* (Boston: Houghton Mifflin, 1901), p. 1. Of the portraits on the east wall of Pennyroyal, only Mark Twain's survives.

90. Wheeler, *Content in a Garden* (Boston: Houghton Mifflin, 1901), pp. 6–9.

91. Wheeler, *Yesterdays,* pp. 283–89, 292, 301–12; William A. Coffin, "J. Carroll Beckwith," *Harpers Weekly* 35 (September 26, 1891), p. 734. Photos of the Beckwith cottage and studio, Archives of American Art, roll 1454; the studio no longer exists.

92. Jeanette Thurber Connor, "A Few Words on Aunt Cannie," *Dedication of Ground for the Candace Wheeler Wild Garden,* Onteora, September 7, 1921, unpaged; J. Russell Harper, *Early Painters and Engravers in Canada* (Toronto: Univ. of Toronto Press, 1970), p. 262; George Reid, address at his retirement as principal of the Ontario College of Art, 1928 (Justine Hommel provided this reference).

93. Diane Galusha, "Pakatakan: An Artist's Haven," *Daily Star,* July 18, 1984; Best, *Ulster and Delaware,* p. 25; McEntee to Mrs. Monnell, May 30, 1886, Archives of American Art. R. Lionel De Lisser, *Picturesque Catskills: Greene County* (Northampton, Mass.: Picturesque Publishing, 1894; reprinted Cornwallville, 1971), p. 69, called Onteora the "most pretentious" of the private parks of Greene County. Whitty Sanford of the Erpf Catskill Cultural Center in Arkville introduced me to the Pakatakan colony.

94. J. Francis Murphy to MacBeth, August 25, 1894, MacBeth Gallery Papers, Archives of American Art; unpublished essay on J. Francis Murphy by Emerson Crosby Kelly, Emerson Crosby Kelly Papers, Archives of American Art; Adah Murphy diary, Emerson Crosby Kelly Papers, Archives of American Art, June 28, 1887, to September 15, 1887.

95. The drawings give Mott's address as 111 Broadway:

Dennis Steadman Francis, *Architects in Practice New York City 1840–1900* (New York: Committee for the Preservation of Architectural Records, 1980), p. 56, indicates Mott was at this address 1887–91.

96. "An Artist's Ideal Home," unidentified newspaper, Emerson Crosby Kelly Papers; Eliot Clark, *J. Francis Murphy* (New York: privately printed, 1926), pp. 16–17; J. Francis Murphy to MacBeth, July 22, 1892, Archives of American Art.

97. Francis Murphy, *J. Francis Murphy: The Landscape Within* (Yonkers: Hudson River Museum, 1982), p. 10; *Paintings and Drawings by J. Francis Murphy* (New York: American Art Association, 1926; reprint of auction catalogue by Olana Gallery, New York, 1978), nos. 68, 85, 119, 246, 248.

98. Kelly in his essay on Murphy outlines the building projects at Arkville. After the turn of the century came a secluded barn studio (1905) for J. Francis and a studio still higher on the hill for his wife.

99. Alfred L. Donaldson, *A History of the Adironacks*, 2 vols. (Port Washington, N.Y.: Ira Friedman, 1963), II, p. 41; Arabella L. Wyant diary, June 30, July 1, 3, 15, 1887 (references furnished by Alice Zigelis, Arkville).

100. A. L. Wyant diary, June 1 and August 30, 1889; *Catalogue of Paintings by the Late A. H. Wyant, N.A.* (New York: Fifth Avenue Art Galleries, 1894; reprinted by Olana Gallery, 1980), no. 50; William H. Gerdts, "American Tonalism," *Tonalism in American Experience* (New York: Grand Central Art Galleries, 1982), p. 24.

101. Wyant's wife, however, may have supplied funds for the house: her diary of October 31, 1888, indicates her interest in buying land from Hoffman. Her sisters Nancy and Mary Locke built an impressive Shingle-style house near the Wyants.

102. Wallace Bruce, *The Hudson* (New York: Bryant Union, 1913), p. 169; *Catskill Mountains* (Rondout, N.Y.: Ulster and Delaware Railroad, 1891), p. 40.

Other artists with quarters at Arkville included Ernest C. Rost, artist and photographer, who is said to have built his Shingle-style studio in 1884 (destroyed by fire 1886), according to John A. Walsh, "The Fabulous Rosts: Three Generations of Fine Artists 1823–1961," 1982, an unpublished essay made available by Larry Newton of Arkville; and Parker Mann, whose Nestlewood was of Alpine style, perhaps stemming from this landscape painter's trip to Switzerland. *Mantle Fielding's Dictionary of American Painters, Sculptors and Engravers* (New York: James F. Carr, 1965), p. 227. Nestlewood's date of contruction is unknown, but James Henry Moser's watercolor of the aesthetic interior is inscribed to Mrs. Mann and dated September 1890. *Quarterly Illustrator* 2 (1894), p. 378, identifies Arthur Parton as residing "in his 'Nestlewood' cottage." On Parton, see the *Dictionary of American Biography*, which describes him as a friend of Wyant and Murphy.

Landscape painter Thomas B. Craig had a board-and-batten house and a rustic studio in Woodland Valley, some twenty miles east of Arkville and not far from the Ulster and Delaware Railroad. Craig's painting of the house is dated 1894 (private collection). Conversation with Alf Evers, 1984; *New York Times*, September 2, 1924.

103. Evers, *Catskills*, pp. 614–18; Karal Ann Marling, *Woodstock: An American Art Colony* (Poughkeepsie: Vassar College Art Gallery, 1977); Poultney Bigelow, "The Byrdcliffe Colony of Arts and Crafts," *American Homes and Gardens* 6 (October 1909), p. 392.

Chronology

1823   Catskill Mountain House built near Haines Falls.

1825   Thomas Cole's first visit to the Catskill Mountains to paint.

1834   George Harvey builds Woodbank at Hastings-on-Hudson.

1836   Cole marries Maria Bartow and settles in her family house, Cedar Grove, near Catskill.

1841   Robert Havell, Jr., moves to Sing Sing (now Ossining) and builds Rocky Mount.

1844   Frederic E. Church begins two years of study with Cole in his home at Catskill.

1846   Cole designs and builds an Italianate studio on his property.

1847   Samuel F. B. Morse purchases Locust Grove in Poughkeepsie.

1848   Asher B. Durand, John F. Kensett, John W. Casilear, and Joseph Vollerming board at Palenville and paint in the surrounding area.

Thomas Cole dies, February 8.

1851 –52   Morse, with the aid of Alexander Jackson Davis, redesigns Locust Grove as an Italian villa.

1853   Jervis McEntee builds Weinbergh, his studio in Rondout, designed by Calvert Vaux, his brother-in-law.

1860   Church buys land on a ridge near Hudson, opposite Cole's house, and begins to construct a small cottage (Cozy Cottage), designed by Richard Morris Hunt.

Thomas P. Rossiter designs and builds his house in Cold Spring.

1862   Charles Herbert Moore paints Cole's old studio.

1866   Jasper F. Cropsey buys forty-five acres at Warwick.

1866 –67   Albert Bierstadt builds Malkasten at Irvington-on-Hudson, designed by Jacob Wrey Mould.

1867   Church buys the summit of the ridge adjoining his property and commissions Hunt to design a larger house. Hunt is later dismissed.

1869   Cropsey designs and builds a studio-house, Aladdin, at Warwick.

Moore and his family occupy the Lodge, a small cottage of his own design north of the Cole homestead.

1870   Church, in consultation with Vaux, begins to build Olana.

Sanford Gifford builds a studio belvedere atop the family house in Hudson.

1871   George Henry Hall purchases an old store near Palenville and begins to transform it into a studio.

1877   David M. Armstrong begins to make additions to a farmhouse on family property near Newburgh.

1880   George Inness boards with Sarah Hull Hallock at Milton and paints in a nearby barn; he continues to do so for two more summers.

Peekamoose Fishing Club incorporated at Peekamoose Mountain. John Quincy Adams Ward is a member.

1881   Eliza Greatorex buys land at Grassmoor and names her property Chetolah.

1882   Malkasten, Bierstadt's house at Irvington, burns to the ground.

1883   Edward Lamson Henry purchases land at Cragsmoor.

Candace Wheeler and her brother Francis Thurber purchase land north of Tannersville and build houses. (Hers is called Pennyroyal.)

1884   Henry designs and builds a studio-house, Na-Pe-Nia, at Cragsmoor.

Celia Wentworth and her husband build a chalet, the Wigwam, at Peekamoose.

1885   Cropsey buys a board-and-batten house, Ever Rest, at Hastings-on-Hudson, and builds a studio (similar in design to the one at Aladdin, though smaller).

Ward alters the stone house at Peekamoose and constructs a studio.

1886   Peter Hoffman builds an inn at Pakatakan Mountain, which becomes the focal point of an artists' community.

1887   Wheeler and her family form the Catskill Mountain Camp and Cottage Company at Onteora Park.

J. Francis Murphy buys property adjoining the Hoffman house at Pakatakan and builds the first studio-house, Weedwild.

Wyant builds the Shanty, his first home at Pakatakan.

1888   Church begins designing and constructing the studio wing at Olana. It is completed in 1890.

1889   Wyant constructs a large house at Pakatakan. Edward Loyal Field builds his Edsen there. Parker Mann's Nestlewood was probably constructed the same year.

1890   J. Carroll Beckwith builds a house, the Ledge, at Onteora Park.

1891   Frederick S. Dellenbaugh designs and builds his house, Endridge, at Cragsmoor.

1899   Murphy builds a large house at Pakatakan.

1901   George Inness, Jr., builds the large mansion, Chetolah, at Cragsmoor. Howard Greenley is the architect.

Selected Bibliography

Buff, Barbara. "Cragsmoor, An Early American Art Colony." *Magazine Antiques* 114 (November 1978), pp. 1056–67.

Campbell, Catherine. "Benjamin Bellows Grant Stone: A Forgotten American Artist." *New-York Historical Society Quarterly* 62 (January 1978), pp. 22–42.

Champney, Lizzie W. "Summer Haunts of American Artists." *Century Magazine* 30 (October 1885), pp. 845–60.

Cikovsky, Jr., Nicolai. *The Life and Work of George Inness.* New York: Garland, 1977.

Creese, Walter L. *The Crowning of the American Landscape: Eight Great Spaces and Their Buildings.* Princeton: Princeton University Press, 1985.

De Lisser, R. Lionel. *Picturesque Catskills: Greene County.* Northampton, Mass.: Picturesque Publishing Company, 1894.

————. *Picturesque Ulster.* Kingston, N.Y.: Styles & Bruyn, 1896.

Downing, Andrew Jackson. *The Architecture of Country Houses.* New York: D. Appleton, 1851.

————. *A Treatise on the Theory and Practice of Landscape Gardening.* New York: Riker, Thirne, 1854.

Evers, Alf. *The Catskills: From Wilderness to Woodstock.* Garden City, N.Y.: Doubleday, 1972.

Ferber, Linda S., and William H. Gerdts, Jr. *The New Path: Ruskin and the American Pre-Raphaelites.* Brooklyn: Brooklyn Museum, 1985.

Fort, Ilene Susan. "High Art and the American Experience: The Career of Thomas Pritchard Rossiter." M.A. thesis, Queens College, 1975.

Goss, Peter L. "An Investigation of Olana." Ph.D. dissertation, Ohio University, 1973.

Hendricks, Gordon. *Albert Bierstadt, Painter of the American West.* New York: Harry N. Abrams, 1974.

Huntington, David C. *The Landscapes of Frederic Edwin Church.* New York: George Braziller, 1966.

Howat, John K. *The Hudson River and Its Painters.* New York: The Viking Press, 1972.

Lamb, Martha J. *The Homes of America.* New York: D. Appleton, 1879.

Lillie, Lucy C. "Two Phases of American Art." *Harper's New Monthly Magazine* 80 (January 1889–90), pp. 206–16.

Lossing, Benson J. *The Hudson from the Wilderness to the Sea.* New York: Virtue and Yorston, 1866.

McCausland, Elizabeth. *The Life and Work of Edward Lamson Henry, N.A. 1841–1919.* Albany: University of the State of New York, 1945.

Maddox, Kenneth W. *In Search of the Picturesque: Nineteenth Century Images of Industry along the Hudson River Valley.* Contemporary site photographs by Douglas Baz. Annandale-on-Hudson, N.Y.: Edith C. Blum Art Institute, 1983.

Mann, Maybelle. *Walter Launt Palmer.* Exton, Pa.: Schiffer, 1984.

Markus, Julia. "Jasper Cropsey's Resonant Rooms Come to Life Again," *Smithsonian* (January 1980), pp. 104–11.

Moore, Charles Herbert. "Materials for Landscape Art in America." *Atlantic Monthly* (November 1889), pp. 670–81.

Morse, Samuel F. B. *Lectures on the Affinity of Painting with the Other Fine Arts.* Columbia, Mo.: University of Missouri Press, 1983.

Murphy, Francis. *J. Francis Murphy: The Landscape Within.* Yonkers, N.Y.: Hudson River Museum, 1982.

Noble, Lewis Legrand. *The Life and Works of Thomas Cole.* Cambridge, Mass.: Harvard University Press, 1964.

Novak, Barbara. *American Painting of the Nineteenth Century: Realism, Idealism, and the American Experience.* New York: Praeger, 1971.

O'Brien, Raymond J. *American Sublime: Landscape and Scenery of the Lower Hudson Valley.* New York: Columbia University Press, 1981.

Parra, Kaycee Benton. *The Works of E. L. Henry: Recollections of a Time Gone By.* Shreveport, La.: R. W. Norton Art Gallery, 1987.

Scott, John. "The Hill Family of Clarksville." *South of the Mountains* 19 (January–March 1975), pp. 5–18

Sharp, Lewis I. *John Quincy Adams Ward: Dean of American Sculpture.* Newark, Del.: University of Delaware Press, 1985.

Shelley, Donald A. "George Harvey and His Atmospheric Landscapes of North America." *New-York Historical Society Quarterly* 32 (April 1948), pp. 104–13.

Stebbins, Theodore E. *The Hudson River School: Nineteenth Century American Landscapes in the Wadsworth Atheneum.* Hartford, Conn.: Wadsworth Atheneum, 1976.

Talbot, William S. *Jasper F. Cropsey 1823–1900.* New York: Garland, 1977.

Tuckerman, Henry T. *Book of the Artists: American Artist Life.* 1867; reprinted New York: James F. Carr, 1966.

Van Zandt, Roland. *The Catskill Mountain House.* New Brunswick: Rutgers University Press, 1966.

Vaux, Calvert. *Villas and Cottages.* New York: Harper, 1857.

Webster, J. Carson. *Erastus Dow Palmer.* Newark, Del.: University of Delaware Press, 1983.

Weir, John Ferguson. "The Recollections of John Ferguson Weir," ed. by Theodore Sizer. *New-York Historical Society Quarterly* 41 (April 1957), pp. 109–41.

Weiss, Ila S. *Sanford Robinson Gifford (1823–1880).* New York: Garland, 1977.

Wheeler, Candace. *Yesterdays in a Busy Life.* New York: Harper, 1918.

Zukowsky, John, and Robbe Pierce Stimson. *Hudson River Villas.* New York: Rizzoli, 1985.

INDEX